Mountain Bike
Adventures in™

SOUTHWEST
BRITISH COLUMBIA
50 RIDES

Mountain Bike Adventures in™

SOUTHWEST BRITISH COLUMBIA

50 RIDES

GREG MAURER
WITH TOMAS VRBA

**THE
MOUNTAINEERS**

Published by
The Mountaineers
1001 SW Klickitat Way, Suite 201
Seattle, WA 98134

CV
1046
.C22
B755
1999

First edition, 1999

Published simultaneously in Great Britain by Cordee, 3a DeMontfort Street, Leicester, England, LE1 7HD

Manufactured in the United States of America

Edited by Christine Clifton-Thornton
Maps by Jacqulyn Weber
Elevation profile charts by Tomas Vrba
All photographs by Greg Maurer unless otherwise noted
Cover and book design by Jennifer Shontz
Layout by Jennifer Shontz

Cover photograph: *Gun Creek to Spruce Lake, Southern Chilcotin, British Columbia*
Frontispiece: *Contributor Tomas Vrba gaining air near Botanie Mountain, Lillooet*

Library of Congress Cataloging-in-Publication Data
   Maurer, Greg.
     Mountain bike adventures in southwest British Columbia / Greg
Maurer with Tomas Vrba. — 1st ed.
     p.   cm.
   "Published simultaneously in Great Britain by Cordee, 3a
DeMontfort Street, Leicester, England."

   Includes bibliographical references.
   ISBN 0-89886-628-6 (paper)
   1. All terrain cycling—British Columbia—Guidebooks. 2. British
Columbia—Guidebooks. I. Vrba, Tomas. II. Title.
   GV1046.C22 B755 1998
   796.6'3'097113—dc21
                                 99-6060
                                  CIP

Contents

CHILLIWACK RIVER VALLEY

SIMILKAMEEN

LILLOOET

SOUTHERN CHILCOTIN

Gonzo technical forest riding on the Thrill Me Kill Me trail option

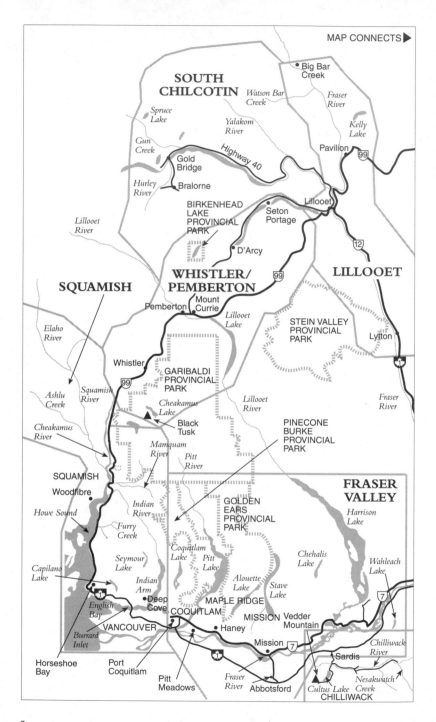

SOUTH CHILCOTIN

Big Bar Creek

Watson Bar Creek

Fraser River

Spruce Lake

Yalakom River

Kelly Lake

Gun Creek

Highway 40

Pavilion

99

Gold Bridge

Hurley River

Bralorne

Lillooet

BIRKENHEAD LAKE PROVINCIAL PARK

Seton Portage

Lillooet River

D'Arcy

12

WHISTLER/ PEMBERTON

LILLOOET

99

SQUAMISH

Pemberton

Mount Currie

Lillooet Lake

STEIN VALLEY PROVINCIAL PARK

Lytton

Elaho River

Whistler

99

GARIBALDI PROVINCIAL PARK

Lillooet River

Fraser River

Ashlu Creek

Squamish River

Cheakamus Lake

Black Tusk

Cheakamus River

Mamquam River

Pitt River

PINECONE BURKE PROVINCIAL PARK

FRASER VALLEY

SQUAMISH

Woodfibre

Indian River

GOLDEN EARS PROVINCIAL PARK

Harrison Lake

Howe Sound

Furry Creek

Coquitlam Lake

Pitt Lake

Chehalis Lake

Wahleach Lake

Capilano Lake

Seymour Lake

Alouette Lake

Stave Lake

7

Indian Arm

Deep Cove

MAPLE RIDGE

English Bay

COQUITLAM

MISSION

Vedder Mountain

Chilliwack River

Burrard Inlet

VANCOUVER

Haney

Mission

7

Sardis

Horseshoe Bay

Port Coquitlam

Pitt Meadows

Fraser River

Abbotsford

Cultus Lake

Nesakwatch Creek

CHILLIWACK

8

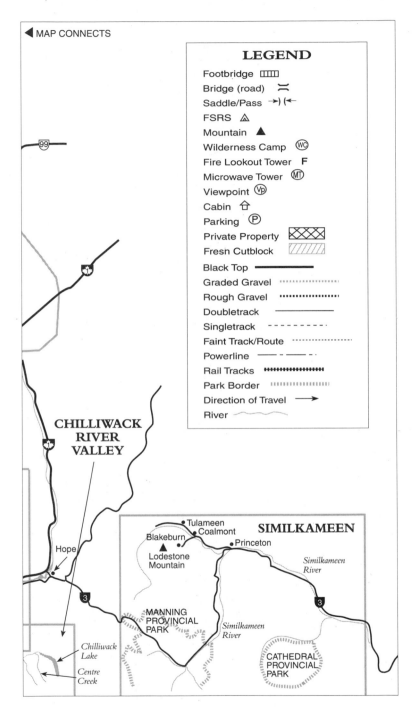

LEGEND

Footbridge ⅢⅢ
Bridge (road) ≍
Saddle/Pass →)(←
FSRS ⚠
Mountain ▲
Wilderness Camp Ⓦ©
Fire Lookout Tower **F**
Microwave Tower Ⓜ®
Viewpoint Ⓥ℗
Cabin ⌂
Parking Ⓟ
Private Property ⬛
Fresn Cutblock ▨

Black Top ▬▬▬
Graded Gravel ·················
Rough Gravel ●●●●●●●●●●●●●
Doubletrack ———
Singletrack - - - - - - -
Faint Track/Route ·················
Powerline — · — · —
Rail Tracks ●●●●●●●●●●●●●
Park Border ······················
Direction of Travel ⟶
River ～～～～

CHILLIWACK
RIVER
VALLEY

Tulameen
Coalmont
Blakeburn
SIMILKAMEEN
Princeton
Lodestone
Mountain
Hope
Similkameen
River
MANNING
PROVINCIAL
PARK
Similkameen
River
Chilliwack
Lake
CATHEDRAL
PROVINCIAL
PARK
Centre
Creek

Preface

Southwest British Columbia offers tremendous opportunities for mountain bike adventures. The goal of this guide is to provide the necessary information for cyclists to explore the best mountain biking British Columbia has to offer. Our aim is to get mountain bikers out of the city to experience great outback riding, combining some of the best singletrack and primitive road this part of the province has to offer. The rides detailed in this guide have been selected for their natural attributes and riding quality. Gaining familiarity with the region and the wealth of rideable terrain that is covered in this book will satisfy your wanderlust and perhaps prompt you to explore further.

Seven regions within four hours of travel from Vancouver are described here. Alpine destinations, hidden lakes, hot springs and canyons, old-growth groves, wild rivers, and historic places all give flavor to this guide. Cyclists of all abilities, from neophytes to the experienced, will find routes that will entice them to seek their own adventure.

Adventure is not without ethics. As mountain cyclists we have an ethical responsibility to the environment, other users, and ourselves. Travel in mountain areas should be made with as little impact as possible. Leave minimal evidence of your passage and be respectful of mountain ecology. Hikers and other users have the right of way, so dismount. Having a conscientious and thoughtful attitude will go a long way toward preserving our ability to use trails in the future. Almost all of the riding in this guide is on public or park land. Be aware of private land and stick to the described routes. As a final note, be accountable to yourself, be safe, wear a helmet, and be prepared for the worst weather. In case of an emergency, knowing rudimentary first aid at the very least will be an asset, for help may take time in arriving.

With exploration, your awareness and sensitivity to the environment will likely increase. This guide may also stimulate your conscience. In some areas, wilderness values are being compromised by industry. If you don't like what you see, get involved. Change can only occur if you speak out. Ultimately I hope that you use this book as a tool for discovery and that you learn not only of the country but of yourself. The mountain bike is the perfect vehicle for accomplishing this goal.

Acknowledgments

Of course, this guide could not have been written without the help of many people, especially Tomas Vrba, whose enthusiasm, penchant for detail, and heart for discovery serve this guide well.

Special thanks go out to: Dan and Lee Gerak, Pitt Lake Resorts; Chris Laustraup at Sea Trek; Mike Blenkarn and Jeremy Guard at Arc'teryx; Brian Benson at Cybersports; Dalton McArthur, Bernie Ivanco, Graham Seefeldt, Allison Baguley, George Ralph, John Tisdale, Randy Atkinson, Tim Ryan, Kevin McLane, Lyle Knight, Garnet Mierou, Kevin Healy; Matt, Chris, Merv and Kathy Parr, and Dad and Mom for special support; Mary Ellen Hanlon, Lynn Mutrie, Debbie Rand, Kerry Ann Dawson, and Margaret Wilson; Mark and Julie Obsniuk, Ian Ferch for his intrepidness, Mr. and Mrs. Vrba for help and support; Mark Bitz, Steve Threndyle, Mike Thompson, and Robert Tomich, who have over the years shared the love of wild places and big adventures, and especially to Greg Stoltmann, for spending stoic time in the far reaches of the Chilcotin when no one else would; and special thanks to Dawn Hanna for syntax and Richard Thomas Wright for inspiration.

Finally, I'd like to thank Margaret Foster and the staff at Mountaineers Books for believing in this project, and especially Christine Ummel for time spent organizing the final product.

Adventure

The uncertainty in the attainment of a goal can cause fear, it's normal.
Thrive on uncertainty and discover the unknown,
Act with spirit,
Drive on. Don't compromise yourself by accepting the mediocre,
Explore the land, explore the potential,
Venture into wild. Be bold.

Seize the challenge, savor it, embrace it,
Grow with it. Risk for success, for inspiration.
Adventure . . . live naked.

Carpe Diem
G. Maurer, 1999

Fording upper Furry Creek in November flood

Introduction

ON THE TRAIL

Off-road trails and the wilderness experience are a public resource to share and preserve. Common sense and the use of conscientious etiquette go a long way in making mountain biking acceptable. Inconsiderate actions on the trail will paint all mountain riders with the same negative brush. Land managers need little reason to close trails. Do not give them any reasons. Being respectful and responsible will enhance our position in the trail community. Obey signs, close cattleguards, and respect aboriginal and private land.

Hikers and equestrian traffic make up the bulk of other trail users. Horses are easily spooked by bikes. When this happens there is a threat to the horseback rider's safety. If an inexperienced wrangler is involved, the results could be disastrous. It is the biker's responsibility to dismount and yield. When encountering hikers, you should have the same attitude. You must ride in a safe and courteous manner so that others perceive your impact to be minimal, both to them and the environment. Avoid speeding and warn others when approaching from behind. The sheer joy of being able to explore the mountains with a bike is in itself exciting. It is celebratory of the wilderness experience. We are incredibly lucky to live in this part of the world; just being here is a privilege. The natural attributes are phenomenal. Respect the land. Mountain biking can impact the environment, so keep on the trails. Off-trail riding kills plants, and skidding on steep hills causes erosion, as does cutting switchbacks. The biosphere in alpine areas is especially fragile. If you do not have a deep regard for the natural environment, stay home.

Potential hazards exist everywhere. The more difficult trails present greater mishap potential. If you find a section of a trail is too difficult, get off and walk the hard part. Common-sense precautions will go a long way toward avoiding mishaps. Be aware of wildlife and keep an eye out for ORVs (off-road vehicles), four-by-four's, and ATVs (all-terrain vehicles). Hikers and horses especially will require that you display the best in trail etiquette, for their safety as well as your own.

Support Cycling B.C. This is an umbrella organization for all bike clubs in British Columbia and is active in both trail enhancement and advocacy. Become involved and take action to protect mountain biking rights.

International Mountain Bicycling Association Trail Rules

1. Ride on open trails only
2. Leave no trace
3. Control your bike
4. Always yield the trail to other users
5. Never spook animals
6. Plan ahead

BEING PREPARED

Fitness Level

To enjoy mountain biking to the fullest, one should come into the sport with an average fitness level. The easiest rides in this guide can be done with an average fitness level and little experience. If you already cycle, you will be familiar with the rigors of elevation gain and know your limits. Of course, these limits can be expanded by riding regularly on trails that gradually increase in difficulty. Neophytes who have not cycled before should spend some time riding to increase their stamina before attempting the more advanced trails in this guide. Try some rides with minimal elevation gain before you push yourself beyond your present limits. Any sport takes preparation, and with the offroad nature of mountain biking it is especially so. Be patient and develop your skills. Know your bike and the terrain before you commit to longer rides. Partner with more experienced riders to learn the finer points of off-road travel. Riding on a regular basis will provide adequate training to help increase your overall stamina, physical fitness, and skill level.

Clothing and Gear

Clothing. Functional best describes what you should look for in clothing. Mountain biking can be an extremely active sport, and sweat should be expected. You need gear that will dry quickly, keep you warm or cool, and be lightweight. Recent technology has honed synthetic clothing to a fine edge. Lycra, poly fibers, Capilene, Lifa, Microft, Gore-Tex, Simplex, and a variety of other brands rule the outdoor clothing market. Some shells made out of fabrics such as Gore-Tex or Microft are both waterproof and breathable.

Because you'll be working hard, you'll want your first layer to be lightweight polypropylene. A layer of fleece or pile can be added for warmth. A breathable shell can be added as a final layer that will act as a wind break and shed wet weather. Consider wearing a waterproof pant with slim or adjustable pant legs that won't catch in the chain ring.

On shorter rides of a day or less you can afford to go lighter, but on longer rides make sure you are prepared. Mountain weather is change-able, so expect the worst. If a squall hits, if your bike breaks down, or if you're injured, you'll need all the help you can get. Always carry extra layers of warm clothing. Hypothermia is a serious concern; see "Hypothermia" in the Health and Nutrition section.

Helmet. Before starting out, don't forget your helmet. This impor-tant piece of gear should always be worn while riding. If you manage to fall off your bike, you'll be hitting the ground at 24 km/hr (15 mph), and that's without the bike moving. Add a bit of speed to the equa-tion, and the answer could be traumatic.

The best helmets have a hard shell over a styrofoam core. These lightweight helmets, often with a sun visor, are a bit more expensive than varieties without the hard shell, but they're worth it. Every hel-met should be retired after an impact, or if fractures develop in the styrofoam.

Helmets should be approved by the American National Standards Institute or the Canadian Standards Association, or certified by the Snell Memorial Foundation. Don't leave home without it.

Riding shoes. Clipless riding shoes are great but wear quickly when used off the bike. You may want to consider a durable hiking/riding shoe and pedals with toe clips if you plan to travel off your steel steed. A variety of waterproof coverings are available to keep your feet dry. Extra wool socks will increase your comfort level if your feet get wet and cold.

Overnight gear. On overnight trips, mountain biking becomes a hybrid of two sports: backpacking and cycle touring. Everything you need to survive is either packed in your panniers, attached to your racks, or on your back. The old mountaineering axiom to "go fast and light" applies even more to mountain bike touring.

Bolt a sturdy rack to the bike's rear triangle to accommodate pan-niers. Consider a front rack for longer trips, but keep in mind a heavy load will cause sluggish steering. Small panniers are best, to minimize the load. Consider using only one in the back for weekend trips, placed on the uphill side so it won't interfere if you have to get off and push.

Extended trips will require an internal 30- to 50-liter backpack. Load the heavy stuff on the bike: tools, stove, fuel, sleeping bag, foam pad, and food. Lighter items, such as extra clothing, can go in your backpack. Bungee cords and a couple of carabiners will aid in attach-ing the load to the bike. You'll want a tight unit that doesn't rattle over every root.

On technical terrain, keep the bike light and put the extras in your backpack. On logging roads and doubletrack, put everything on the bike, including your pack. Bring the lightest stove possible and carry minimal fuel.

For shelter, take the lightest tent possible. If you are really weight conscious, consider a bivy sack or tarp. A good weather forecast with high pressure can be your best ally.

WHAT TO BRING
First-aid Kit

Remember that mountain bike trails in southwest British Columbia can be very remote. Rescue can be a long way off. Do not count on rescue; be prepared to be self-sufficient. Carry a small, lightweight first-aid kit that contains the following:

Ibuprofen for aches and pains
Sunscreen
Elastic bandage for knees and ankle sprains
Butterfly bandages for closing deep wounds

The Bare Essentials

Always carry with you the bare essentials, no matter how long you plan to be out riding.

Bear spray
Common sense
Compass/altimeter
Extra food
First-aid kit
Headlamp
Lighter in a container, fire starter
Map in a self-sealing plastic baggie
Space blanket or orange garbage bag
Sunglasses, especially in alpine environs (eye shields)
Trail guide
Water
Waterbottles
Wool hat or toque

Tool and Repair Checklist

Be sure your bike is in the best shape it can be and is tuned from top to bottom before heading out on a trip. Know it well. If you know how to do a complete overhaul of the bike yourself, all the better.

Learning how to break chain in the upper Yalakom Valley

The more technical skill you have, the better equipped you'll be to handle yourself and your bike out on the trail.

Keep in mind that walking a wounded bike loaded with camping gear is tough. Breakdowns that you cannot fix can cause a mental breakdown. Self-doubt, recrimination, and existential agony can torture the ill prepared—so be prepared. A tool and repair kit at minimum should include the following:

Allen keys
Duct tape
Extra brake and gear cables
Multi-tool "cool tool" with chainbreaker
Oil
Small rag
Spare derailleur
Spare tube
Swiss Army knife
Tire patch kit
Tire pump
Wire

Clothing Checklist
Breathable waterproof pants
Breathable waterproof windbreaker

Fleece pants (seasonal option)
Fleece top, mid- and heavy-weight
Gloves—padded or wool
Helmet
Long tights
Padded shorts or quick dry nylon shorts
Polypropylene layers
Stream-crossing shoes
Waterproof over-mitts
Wool socks

Overnight Checklist
Panniers
Tarp, tent, or bivy sack
Sleeping bag
Sleeping pad
Lightweight stove and fuel
Cooking gear
Extra food
Extra socks
Toilet paper
Mosquito netting if needed
Plastic garbage bags or dry bag
Waterproof stuff sacks
Rope for hanging food
Bungee cords
Snap-link carabiner

HELPFUL HINTS FOR EFFICIENT TRAVEL

Fine-tune your bike so that all adjustments to the seat post, pedals, and handlebars ensure the workload is evenly distributed over all muscle groups to reduce muscular fatigue. The idea is to be able to grind efficiently and comfortably. The geometry of most mountain bikes sets the rider in a slightly tucked position for maximum control on rough terrain. Make sure your mountain bike fits your body size. A good way to find out if the bike frame is sized right is to straddle the top tube on your bike. If your crotch is between 5 and 10 centimeters from the tube, you're okay.

There are three types of pedals from which to choose. The choice is purely personal. Regular pedals are not recommended, because your foot can easily slip off the pedal during technical maneuvers. Toe clips act as a trap for your foot, and are a better choice. They support the foot and give power to the upstroke. In addition, they help prevent the foot from slipping off the pedal. Novices are encouraged to try this system before considering clipless pedals. Clipless pedals fasten onto the shoe and help the rider become one with the bike, literally. These pedals also give support and aid during the upstroke but are more expensive, requiring special shoes and pedal spindles. Releasing your feet from the pedals takes practice. The release is adjustable, but ankle injuries and crashes can occur if the system doesn't release properly. Whether the shoes will withstand the rigors of hiking, stream crossings, et cetera, is another question you might want to consider. For racers, this type of pedal may be advantageous, but if you are thinking of abusing your shoe on the trail, this system may not be a good idea.

Having the optimum leg stance is important for efficiency. Adjust the seat post and saddle so that your thighs on the upstroke are never horizontal. Make sure your forward knee is centered over the forward pedal spindle when you're in motion. The pedal crank should be parallel to the ground. This will align leg muscles for smooth, efficient pedaling. The ball of your foot should always be centered mid–pedal with the foot kept level. At the top of the pedal stroke, the thigh should be sloped downward to increase your power stroke. At the bottom of the pedal stroke, make sure that both the knee and ankle are never fully extended, and remember to never lock your knees or ankles.

A correct upper body and back position will ensure comfortable and quick reactive handling of your mountain bike. Back strain will be reduced if your hands reach the handlebars with ease. You'll want to be in a comfortable stance with your arms extended, so that your body doesn't hunch over the handlebars. Freedom of neck movement for the ability to look ahead is important. If you find that your neck and back are getting sore, it's likely you are leaning too far forward.

Singletrack or rough-road riding will be more manageable if the body is tucked so that the weight is positioned over the front wheel. Handling and reaction time will also be more efficient and effective.

Relaxed arms are an asset in controlling your bike. Never lock the elbows; instead, bend them slightly. When moving over technical ground try to remain fluid. Be at one with your bike. Make sure you do not feel cramped, stretched, or uncomfortable.

HEALTH AND NUTRITION
Hypothermia
Hypothermia is one of the greatest killers of the outdoors. When your body core cools, your thinking and reflexes slow. You tend to

Rehydrating above Leon Creek on the Watson Bar Loop

make stupid mistakes that can further jeopardize your position. If you are wet, the onset of hypothermia is faster. If you've been pushing hard and you haven't eaten enough, you can be even more susceptible to cold. Be aware of how your body feels. Once you become chilled, it is difficult for the body to recover; regaining body warmth is much harder than losing it. Dress accordingly and use common sense. A wool hat or toque can be a life saver.

Hyperthermia

At the other end of the spectrum is hyperthermia. With summer weather and drier environments comes the potential for over-heating. To avoid this condition, be sure to rest. Drink plenty of water before, during, and after a ride. Try to keep cool and bring a brimmed hat for after the ride. On hot days, avoid clothing made with fabric such as polypropylene, which wicks moisture away from the body. Sweat helps cool the body, so consider cotton clothing, which holds moisture in. You may even want to soak your shirt to keep cool.

Remember, the elements are harsh and not to be taken for granted. Your body is fragile and cannot easily endure extremes at either end of the spectrum. Use common sense.

Water

Mountain biking is an active sport, so drink lots of water to keep hydrated. Your body will perspire and rid itself of moisture through every breath you exhale. Before you head out on the trail, drink at least a liter of water, especially in the summer, and replenish frequently. Thirst is not an accurate gauge of hydration; drink before you get thirsty. If your urine is clear, you are adequately hydrated. Gatorade or other sport drink additives are good for energy and body salt replacement.

In areas where animal and human populations abound, the water may be suspect. This is especially pronounced in interior regions where cattle grazing occurs. Bring water with you or filter what is available. Even better, for overnight trips when you carry a stove, consider boiling water for five minutes. This will kill all harmful bacteria.

Food

For trail food, think high-energy, concentrating on foods that the body can metabolize quickly. Consider carbo-loading before your ride so your body has an initial store to draw upon. Pizza and pasta are great pre-ride body fuels. During the ride, snack on fresh or dried bananas (nature's little power bars), fig bars, chocolate, or hard candies to provide a quick energy fix.

For overnight trips, consider packing pasta, potato flakes, and dehydrated veggies, chicken, and sauces, along with powdered soups with noodles to augment your diet.

WEATHER AND ROUTE FINDING
Weather

Travel in the outdoors is dictated by one major element—weather. The southwest corner of British Columbia is influenced by weather patterns that originate over the Pacific Ocean. Frontal storm systems of low pressure carry clouds heavy with moisture, which deposit the bulk of the precipitation along the coast. As the heavy clouds are forced to clear the barrier of the coastal mountains, they lose moisture. Meteorologists call this orographic precipitation. The interior regions of Whistler/Pemberton, the Southern Chilcotin, Lillooet, and Similkameen all receive reduced rainfall compared to their coastal counterparts—Squamish, the Fraser Valley, and the Chilliwack River Valley.

Storm cells frequently originate in the southwest. As frontal systems leave, recalcitrant showers can linger in the mountains even after the bulk of a storm blows through. Be aware of trail erosion during the rainy season, from October to April.

May, June, July, August, and September are the driest months. October tends to be a transitional month before the first snow arrives at higher elevations in November.

Expect the wettest weather from November through winter to early spring. Most winters feature extended bouts of high pressure, which result in stable good weather. If you have the tenacity to brave the cool, clear air and the accompanying winds, you can be rewarded with some great riding, especially at elevations below 500 meters. Snow at sea level is not common in the coastal regions, but when it does occur, it usually doesn't last. Inland, freezing temperatures in winter produce snowlines above 500 meters. During winter it may be a challenge to find good snow-free riding. Warmer coastal regions are the best bet. For other regions, you'll have to wait for spring.

While coastal regions are tempered by the warming influence of the ocean, the interior is not. Interior and mountain areas are higher in elevation and have lower winter and early spring temperatures. This translates into more snowfall as storms move inland. Don't consider riding in the interior before May unless the rides are at lower elevations.

Summer weather tends to be more stable in the interior than on the coast. Weather systems coming from the ocean take longer to penetrate the natural boundary of the coastal mountains. As a result, temperatures are higher and the climate drier in the interior lowlands than on the coast. For example, in the Lillooet region, in the interior, the summer environment is very dry and almost desertlike, while on the coast the climate is humid and moisture-loving conifer forests cover the landscape.

All mountain areas in every region are susceptible to sudden

Downhill powder slaloming in the first deep alpine snow of winter © Tomas Vrba

weather changes. Summer valley heating can cause localized mountain squalls. It's not unusual in mountain regions to experience lightning, hail, snow, winds, and low clouds, sometimes all in a single day. Keep in mind that low clouds associated with unstable mountain weather may complicate route finding.

Multi-colored rings around the sun, often called "sun dogs," can indicate moisture in the air and a possible weather change within a day or so. High, towering cumulus clouds can also indicate changing weather. These may evolve into dark thunderheads, which could mean an approaching lightning storm. Lenticular streaming can sometimes be seen on top of high peaks and cumulus clouds. These long, thin, lens-shaped clouds indicate high, upper-level winds that may be the precursor to inclement weather.

Route Finding

Using the mountain bike as an adventure tool is like taking hiking to the next step. You are in the mountain environment basically unassisted, so the same rules apply. Be prepared. Take the essentials for survival with you regardless of the length of the trip. Maps are a requisite for backcountry travel, as is a compass. Knowing how to use them is essential. Maps in this guide are meant only for basic orientation and to give you an indication of the routes; study supplementary maps of the area beforehand, and on every ride bring with you a topographic map that covers your route. Aside from being essential tools for navigation, maps can be helpful to denote your place on the landscape and identify distant features located off the maps in this book. Government-issue topographic maps are quite accurate; 1:50,000 scale is the most detailed. Larger-scale B.C. Forest Service regional recreation maps show rough detail of the drainages, roads, and campsites. For information on getting the maps you need, see the "Maps" section later in this chapter.

An altimeter can help tell you where you are as well as indicate changing weather. It's an excellent orienteering device. Some sport watches incorporate them into their design. If you stay at the same elevation but the altimeter shows a rise in elevation, then you know the barometric pressure has dropped. This can mean bad weather is on the way. If the altimeter shows a drop in elevation, the barometric pressure has risen and good weather may be on the way.

WILDLIFE

Southwest British Columbia's rugged topography helps harbor a variety of wildlife. Even close to major population centers, wildlife species are well represented. Avian and mammal populations abound. A wide cross-section of bird life can be viewed, from domestic robins and sparrows to raptors, eagles, and hawks. Mammals are profuse, with ground squirrels and alpine pikas at one end of the spectrum and bears, cougars, and moose at the other.

Of note to the biking community, potential hazards exist in mountain areas where larger mammal species reside, especially bear and cougar. Both can be attracted to moving objects, especially if the objects are quiet. Your passage in animal-prone terrain should be noisy enough to give them fair warning of your presence. The best advice is to make sure that the animals hear you before you arrive. Attach a bell to your bike, or let out the occasional joyful whoop while going for that 30-kilometer downhill descent. Keep in mind that some bells sound like marmots; choose carefully. Don't become moving bait.

When sighting bears, make an effort to avoid them. If they refuse to leave, ride elsewhere. Hang food at night away from camp and up high. A full-grown bear on its hind legs can reach in excess of 12 feet. Bears also possess a great olfactory system, so store everything in self-closing baggies and waterproof stuff bags. A 20-liter kayaking dry bag works great. Keep your camp clean.

In the years I've been in the wilderness I've yet to experience a close encounter, even when riding in the depths of the Northwest Territories. Nevertheless, do not let your guard down and always be prepared to make noise. Wild grizzlies and black bears are not especially inquisitive; they want to be left alone. If you encounter a bear, back away slowly and talk in a calm voice. Never turn and run; that will only trigger a bear's innate predator response. If an attack occurs, don't fight back. Curl up into a small ball to protect your internal organs and cover your neck and head with your arms. Bear spray, with the active ingredient Capsicum, is a last resort (in the heat of the moment, try not to stand downwind of the spray). Try to envision yourself looking at a charging sow grizzly with a spray can in your hand!

Much the same attitude holds true for cougars. This elusive cat is present in all regions but in greater concentration in interior dry zones. Cougars will stalk any prey they figure can be easily taken. The cat will seldom attack groups. If you encounter a cougar, try to appear as big and threatening as possible. Make noise. Should an encounter occur, take the opposite tack you would with bears and fight back.

Other large mammals often sighted in this region are moose, bighorn sheep, and wolves. Sightings usually occur from a distance, presenting minimal hazard to the cyclist. Porcupines, another often-spotted mammal, have an irritating propensity to chew on rubber. If you are leaving your bike for any length of time (for instance, to go hiking), hang the wheels. Porcupines seem to be nocturnal so this shouldn't be a problem for day hikers.

There may be small herds of wandering and grazing cattle in the interior rangeland. These docile beasts present no real problems other than being obstacles. However, do not attempt to ride through a herd as their movements can be erratic. Bulls, on the other hand, can be obstinate and should be avoided, but they are rarely seen in the open.

Insects can make summer outdoor existence uncomfortable. They're attracted to areas that have standing water such as pools alongside creeks and swamps. Mosquitoes, black flies, and no-see-ums can make life miserable, so don't forget the repellent.

HOW TO USE THIS GUIDE

To help you select the trails that are right for you, each ride includes a statistical breakdown, a text description, and access information for the approach and the trail itself. In the distance/elevation logs, distances in kilometers and elevations in meters are given along the route, to help give an idea of the level of exertion required (1 kilometer = 0.6211 miles; see "Meters to Feet Equivalents" in the Appendix). An elevation profile is also given as a visual aid for elevation gain. Maps are also included to give an overview of each ride. Short sidebars throughout the book offer tips on bike maintenance, equipment, and safety. And at the end of the book is a table that rates each trail according to difficulty.

While most of the trails in this book are easily bikeable, a few are technically quite difficult and are described as such. A number of routes give access to further backcountry travel and exceptional hikes. The southern Chilcotin is particularly friendly to this type of travel. Mountain bike trips in this guide can usually be done in a day by fit individuals, but consider spending more time, as the scenery is remarkable. This guide is by no means the last statement on the routes available but will provide a starting point for further exploration.

Care has been taken to document all approaches and access, but they can change. The geography of southwest British Columbia's terrain is a mountainous and changing environment. Because of this, a certain amount of change is expected over time. Washouts may occur and new road construction may be cause for some extra routefinding. Information provided in the statistics, text, and distance/elevation logs will help solve any potential directional problems that may arise.

A warped wheel a long way from home, Southern Chilcotin backcountry
©Tomas Vrba

The distance/elevation logs along with the trail elevations will help you know your place on the route at all times. In recording data, it was found that measurements varied to a degree. Differences in odometer model, manufacturer, and calibration of odometer-to-tire sizing all were variables that contributed to slight anomalies in measurement readings. Elevation readings were documented using an altimeter and map. A great deal of time was taken to make these readings as accurate as possible. By using our data while paying attention to landmarks, you won't go wrong.

A trail we've graded as "moderate" may be difficult for some novice riders. Fitness and experience differ among individuals. Negative environmental conditions and full panniers will affect overall output and may make a trail seem more difficult than it might to a rider who is carrying no weight on his bike and who encounters perfect trail conditions. In grading the routes, assessment of every trail has been taken from the standpoint of an average rider with average skills, taking into account both physical and technical difficulty. The rating system uses four categories—easy, moderate, difficult, and advanced—to define the rides. Used in conjunction with all other information presented, it should be easy to choose a trail to fit your particular skill and fitness levels.

Information Blocks

To make trip selection an easy exercise, we have included an information block with eight categories for each trip. Many different qualities influence a ride's overall characteristic. We designed our information blocks to give the rider in a glance a comprehensive view of what to expect when embarking on a biking adventure.

Loop trip/Round trip/Point-to-point: Total kilometers for a trip, whether a loop or a round trip (out-and-back) ride. For point-to-point rides, kilometer distances are noted one way. These rides usually involve the use of a shuttle vehicle.

Duration: Total number of hours needed to complete the ride with few stops for an average fit individual with good route-finding skills. While most rides can be done in the time stated, all areas in this book are aesthetically pleasing and can easily warrant taking extra time to enjoy the surroundings.

Elevation gain: Total overall vertical gain in meters for the entire ride.

High point: Highest point of elevation attained on a particular ride.

Season: Months of the year the trail is typically free of snow. Depends on weather variables and snow pack. Some years are not typical; call before you go to be sure the trail is clear of snow.

Terrain: Route surfaces by type, given in percentages. Terrain surfaces are noted as follows:

BT for Blacktop and paved roads.

GG for Graded Gravel roads that are maintained.

GR for Rough Gravel roads that are ill-maintained.

DT for Doubletrack, primitive or remnant roads that may or may not be four-wheelable.

ST for Singletrack, trails that can only support hiking, horse, or biking traffic.

Rating: This subjective category has been assessed from the standpoint of an average rider with average skills, taking into account both physical and technical difficulty. Ride length may affect the overall rating.

Easy   Few if any natural obstacles (windfall, steep drops), minimal to average elevation gain on non-technical terrain. Neophytes might hike-and-bike rocky sections. The rides with this rating will appeal to novices as well as those with experience who may want an easy spin.

Moderate   Expect obstacles. Some elevation gain, rougher riding surfaces, and longer riding are the norm. Riders with average to intermediate skill levels will have the most fun on these rides. Novices who want to cut their teeth on something harder may hike-and-bike the more challenging sections. Some easy rides can become moderate for their length.

Difficult   More obstacles, more hike-and-biking. More elevation gain, longer riding, and generally rough riding characterize this rating. Riders with average to intermediate skill levels may need to carry their bike or hike-and-bike some of the challenging sections. Some moderate rides can become difficult for their length.

Advanced   All of the above, with the addition of route-finding challenges. Not recommended for novices.

Maps: Serial numbers of government-issue topographic maps are provided so you can purchase the maps you'll need to take with you to aid in travel and supplement the maps in the guide. They provide a detailed overview of the area. The maps that are at 1:50,000 scale—2 centimeters equals 1 kilometer—and 1:250,000 scale—4 centimeters equals 10 kilometers—are the most widely used. These maps may be purchased at retail outlets such as Mountain Equipment Co-op and Geological Survey of Canada in Vancouver (see the "Contacts and Information" section later in this chapter). Or you can order them through Nanaimo Maps at (800) 665-2513. Other supplementary regional recreation maps are available through the B.C. Forest Service. These tend to be at a larger scale but provide good regional overviews that show roads, drainages, and campsites.

CONTACTS AND INFORMATION

Enquiry B.C. (604) 660-2421. This is the single most important number in this book. With it you can be connected to any government agency, provincewide, absolutely free. With this number, you have access to virtually any information you many need. Ask receptionists in provincial government offices about the weather. Ask regional forest service recreation officers about road and trail conditions, weather, flower blooms, access, et cetera. Be creative; it's your tax dollar. From Vancouver and the lower mainland within the 604 area code, dial 660-2421. Elsewhere in British Columbia, dial (800) 663-7867. (Not available in the U.S.)

"We are where?" Orienteering with a topographic map

Emergency Numbers

In an emergency, dial either 911 (not available in all areas) or the Royal Canadian Mounted Police.

Royal Canadian Mounted Police Stations

CHILLIWACK	(604) 792-4611
HOPE	(604) 869-5644
KAMLOOPS	(250) 828-3000
LILLOOET	(250) 256-4244 (NO 911 ACCESS)
MAPLE RIDGE	(604) 463-6251
PEMBERTON	(604) 894-6126 (NO 911 ACCESS)
PRINCETON	(250) 295-6911
SQUAMISH	(604) 898-9611
WHISTLER	(604) 932-3044

Forest Service Contacts

CHILLIWACK	(604) 794-3361 OR (604) 685-5972
KAMLOOPS	(250) 371-3701
LILLOOET	(250) 256-1200
SQUAMISH	(604) 898-2100

Provincial Parks

B.C. PARKS SQUAMISH	(604) 898-3678
B.C. PARKS SUMMERLAND	(250) 494-6500
MANNING PROVINCIAL PARK	(250) 840-8836

Mountain Biking Organizations

CYCLING B.C.
#332 West Broadway
Vancouver, BC V6H 4A9
(604) 737-3034

Topographic Maps

GEOLOGICAL SURVEY OF CANADA
101—605 Robson
Vancouver, BC V6B 5J3
(604) 666-0529

MOUNTAIN EQUIPMENT CO-OP
130 West Broadway
Vancouver, BC V5Y 1P3
(604) 872-7858

NANAIMO MAPS
#8 Church Street
Nanaimo, BC V9R 5H4
(800) 665-2513

Map Libraries

UNIVERSITY OF BRITISH COLUMBIA
2075 Westbrook Mall
Vancouver, BC V6T 1Z1
(604) 822-2231

SIMON FRASER UNIVERSITY
Burnaby Mountain Campus
Burnaby, BC V5A 1S6
(604) 291-4656

Recreation Maps—British Columbia
Forest Service Regional Offices

VANCOUVER FOREST REGION
2100 Labieux Road
Nanaimo, BC V9T 6E9
(800) 331-7001

KAMLOOPS FOREST REGION
515 Columbia Street
Kamloops, BC V2C 2T7
(250) 828-4131

A NOTE ABOUT SAFETY

Safety is an important concern in all outdoor activities. No guidebook can alert you to every hazard or anticipate the limitations of every reader. Therefore, the descriptions of roads, trails, routes, and natural features in this book are not representations that a particular place or excursion will be safe for your party. When you follow any of the routes described in this book, you assume responsibility for your own safety. Under normal conditions, such excursions require the usual attention to traffic, road and trail conditions, weather, terrain, the capabilities of your party, and other factors. Keeping informed on current conditions and exercising common sense are the keys to a safe, enjoyable outing.

—The Mountaineers

SQUAMISH

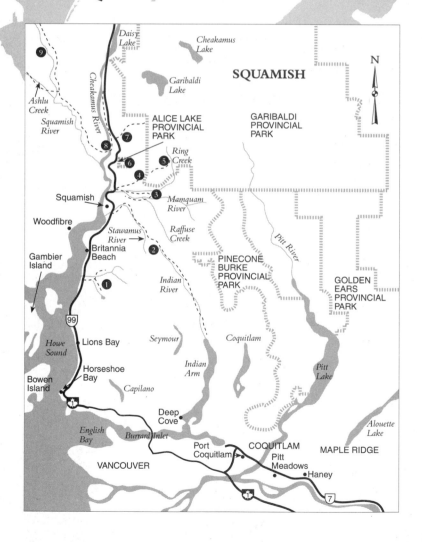

*A*t the end of fjord-like Howe Sound, the growing town of Squamish is the gateway to recreation in the popular Sea to Sky corridor which extends north to Pemberton. Mountain biking is well developed here, with extensive trail systems. Its rising popularity offers yet another outdoor activity to the area, competing with the mainstay sports of rock climbing and windsurfing.

Glaciers have molded the Sea to Sky corridor, from Squamish to Pemberton, into perfect biking terrain. The logging industry has also helped by creating accesses to otherwise inaccessible exploration. The valleys of the Ashlu, Squamish, and Elaho Rivers are roaded, reaching into the deep folds of the Coast Range. Further forays can be made on foot once you've traveled to your destination by bike.

Elfin Lakes represents the best of alpine mountain biking. This classic ride ventures into the southern portion of Garibaldi Provincial Park. It will remain a classic only as long as we don't abuse the privilege and treat hikers with consideration. Always remember to dismount, to allow them safe passage.

Singletrack is also well developed in the Garibaldi Highlands and east of Squamish. Special mention goes to the Ring Creek Rip and Powersmart trails, which deviously combine a system of old skid roads and newly well-built singletrack. The downhill portions are super-exhilarating. The Rip in particular lives up to its name.

The climate in the region is warm, mild, and often wet. The ocean is nearby and modifies all weather. In the mountain valleys, showers can linger after most of a low pressure system has blown through, so dress accordingly.

The rides here are close to Vancouver, scenic, and give a good sense of wilderness. Riding in this region can take place year-round in the valley bottoms and from May to the first snow at higher elevations. The variety of rides in this area appeals to experts and novices alike.

1 MARION AND PHYLLIS LAKES/FURRY CREEK

Round trip: Marion and Phyllis Lakes 16km
     Duration: 4 hours   Season: February to December
Elevation gain: 430m   Terrain: GG30%, RG35%, DT35%
  High point: 480m   Rating: Easy

    Round trip: Furry Creek 20km   Season: February to December
     Duration: 4 hours   Terrain: GG85%, RG15%
Elevation gain: 650m   Rating: Moderate
  High point: 700m   Map: 92-G/11

Despite the close proximity to Vancouver, this area offers two rewarding backcountry adventures. These out-and-back rides will satisfy all
mountain riders from novice to expert. The track to Marion and
Phyllis Lakes is a mellow outing for the beginner or the family that
wants to spend a day cycling. The hanging valley of Furry Creek provides a wilder ride for those who want to cut their teeth on something harder.

    Follow a gated logging road that heads uphill and east beneath the
hydrolines. At 1.5 kilometers, reach a junction and take the south fork

On the Furry Creek bridge, contemplating a deep-pooled swim

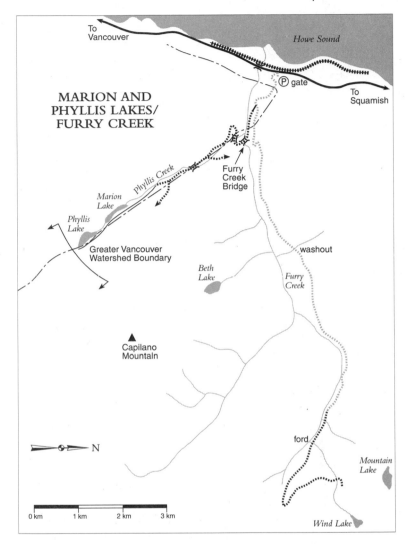

MARION AND
PHYLLIS LAKES/
FURRY CREEK

To Vancouver

Howe Sound

To Squamish

Ⓟ gate

Phyllis Creek

Furry Creek Bridge

Marion Lake

Phyllis Lake

Greater Vancouver Watershed Boundary

washout

Beth Lake

Furry Creek

Capilano Mountain

ford

Mountain Lake

N

Wind Lake

0 km   1 km   2 km   3 km

road to Marion and Phyllis Lakes. The old road runs beneath a canopy of trees for a kilometer before crossing Furry Creek, then climbs a short hill. The remaining 6 kilometers follow open and undulating doubletrack to the lakes and the boundary of the Capilano Watershed. This route is at a low altitude and can be cycled during most winters.

For the steeper Furry Creek drainage, the climb is steady, plateauing only occasionally, to the main height of the hanging valley. At about 600 meters elevation and 2.5 kilometers from the junction, the gradient decreases substantially and the valley opens. Second-growth forest now covers the earlier ravages of old-growth logging. Telltale blue spray paint in some of the remaining Tolkienesque groves hints at more logging to come in the near future. Pedal on. At 10 kilometers, ford upper Furry Creek and continue into wilder terrain. After 12 kilometers or so the road ends.

The gated logging road runs beside the north end of the Furry Creek golf course. The road is only open to mountain bikers and hikers. Further information can be had by phoning the Furry Creek clubhouse for up-to-date conditions: (604) 922-9576. **Note:** In the near future it will also be possible to access via the top of the Furry Creek hill.

APPROACH

From Vancouver and Horseshoe Bay, follow Highway 99 north 26.5 kilometers toward Squamish. Turn right at the Furry Creek Golf Course. Keep left and uphill for 1.5 kilometers to reach a stop sign at a three-way intersection. Make a sharp right turn and park in the pull-out on the side of the gravel road. Be careful not to block the road.

MARION AND PHYLLIS LAKES
DISTANCE/ELEVATION LOG

0km	50m	At the gated road, head uphill.
1.5km	200m	Junction. Take the south fork (right) doubletrack toward Marion and Phyllis Lakes.
2.5km	200m	Furry Creek Bridge.
3.5km	350m	Top of the hill.
8km	430m	Lakes and Greater Vancouver Watershed Boundary.

FURRY CREEK
DISTANCE/ELEVATION LOG

1.5km	200m	Junction. Head left and uphill.
4km	600m	Road plateaus.
6km	600m	Washout.
10km	625m	Ford Furry Creek.
12km	700m	End of the road.

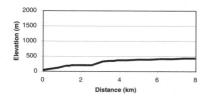

Marion and Phyllis Lakes

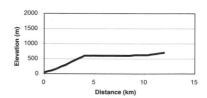

Furry Creek

2 SQUAMISH TO INDIAN ARM

Round trip: 75km
Duration: 6 to 7 hours
Elevation gain: 1,620m
High point: 810m

Season: June to November
Terrain: GG5%, RG95%
Rating: Moderate
Maps: 92-G/11, 92-G/10

Welcome to the ultimate cruise. If you've traveled the Sea to Sky corridor but not looked beyond, this ride will broaden your horizons. This secret passage links two well-known coastal fjords—Indian Arm and Howe Sound.

Most cyclists will have no difficulty in handling the terrain this out-and-back ride delivers. The road surface is mostly smooth, but there is the occasional pothole and the odd rocky section. Intermittent waterbars are the only technical hazard. Some are deep, so watch your speed or you'll end up over the bars and in the bushes. The return trip is about 75 kilometers.

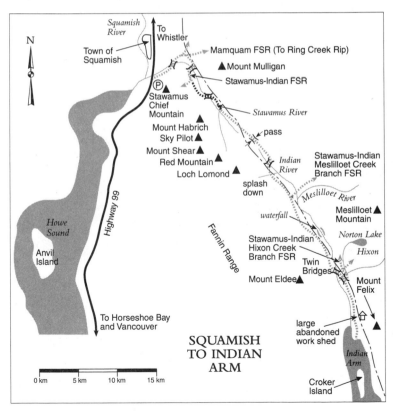

Cruising beside the Indian River estuary, north end of Indian Arm ©Tomas Vrba

The ride begins close to where the Stawamus River flows under Highway 99, and continues east beneath the looming north walls of the Stawamus Chief. A forest of cedar, maple, and alder has grown over the old outwash plain of the Stawamus and Mamquam Rivers. The shade here is welcome on hot, close days and a cool breeze always seems to find its way through the canopy. If that's not refreshing enough, there are plenty of river pools to dip into.

The high point, at about the 12.5-kilometer mark, is 810 meters. For the next 24.6 kilometers, the road drops to sea level, emerging at the estuary where Indian River flows into Indian Arm. Even though there's a log sorting area here, wildlife, including seals, deer, and a variety of marsh birds, still abounds.

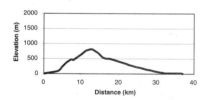

Expect waterfalls and glacier-sculpted terrain on this worthwhile mountain bike tour. Its mellower flavor is a welcome change from other nerve-numbing ventures. Fit riders who go light can complete the return trip in less than eight hours. The potential for exploration may prompt some riders to spend even more time. Several good camp spots can be found en route, especially along the Indian River.

APPROACH

From Horseshoe Bay, follow Highway 99 north toward Squamish. At the north end of Stawamus Chief, about 1 kilometer north of the tourist lookout, turn right on Mamquam Forest Service Road (FSR). Park in the climber's gravel parking lot.

DISTANCE/ELEVATION LOG

0km	0m	From Highway 99, follow Mamquam FSR east along the north walls of Stawamus Chief.
3.8km	90m	Turn right after the 3-mile sign onto Shannon–Indian FSR and start climbing.
5.2km	240m	Turn left onto Stawamus–Indian FSR and climb up the steep valley.
7.1km	450m	Cross the Stawamus River. The upper section of the valley starts to level as it heads up to the pass.
12.5km	810m	Ride through the pass between Stawamus and Indian River. For the next 25.5km, enjoy a casual descent down to Indian Arm.
17km	500m	Splash down through a small creek.
23.3km	270m	Stay right at the STAWAMUS–INDIAN MESLILLOET CREEK BRANCH FSR sign.
27.3km	150m	Stop and view the deep granite gorge and a spectacular waterfall.
31.3km	40m	Cross the Indian River to its east side via a twin bridge. Ride through several cutblocks.
32.6km	30m	Stay right at the STAWAMUS–INDIAN HIXON CREEK BRANCH FSR sign.
35.6km	15m	Pass by a large abandoned work shed.
37.1km	0m	Road ends at the north end of Indian Arm. Retrace your tracks to Squamish.

OPTION: LOOP RIDE

If water transport up Indian Arm can be arranged, a long but adventurous loop ride can be made. Start in either Squamish or Vancouver. About 115 kilometers in all.

3 RING CREEK RIP

Loop trip:	36km	Season:	April to October
Duration:	2 to 3 hours	Terrain:	GG35%, RG5%, ST60%
Elevation gain:	700m	Rating:	Rip, Moderate; Powerhouse
High point:	600m		Plunge option, Difficult
		Maps:	92–G/11, 92–G/12

Hold on to the bars and have the brakes at the ready, because the Rip will have you flying down the trail at warp speed. This exciting singletrack descends an ancient (10,000-year-old) lava flow between

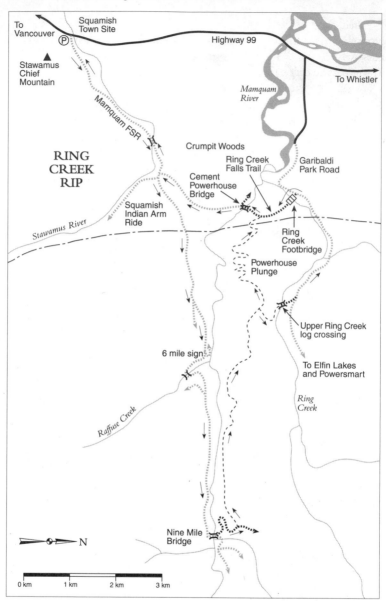

the Mamquam River and Ring Creek. This loop has seen extensive trail work to clear windfall and other debris, and has the added option of connecting to the great technical singletrack of the Powerhouse Plunge. The basalt base can endure a high volume of riders. This route is the latter part of the annual Test of Metal mountain bike race.

Pedal up Mamquam FSR for 15 kilometers to the Nine Mile Br
cross the river, and grind left up Lava Flow Hill to top out bene
narrow, alder-canopied skid road. Get ready for a wild descent.
Travel past abandoned vehicles and at about 21 kilometers, turn left for

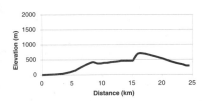

the challenging and sustained technical singletrack of the Powerhouse Plunge. Expect steep switchbacking corners and steep drops before it plateaus through a verdant forest with an almost surreally soft green understory. If this isn't your cup of tea and you want to continue the high-speed Rip, you'll end up at the log crossing at Ring Creek before emerging on Garibaldi Park Road.

Both routes end near the cement bridge at the powerhouse. From Garibaldi Park the way is a bit more circuitous, traveling downhill 3 kilometers to the Ring Creek Falls Trail and footbridge following south to the exit of the Powerhouse Plunge. The routes connect and head farther south to Mamquam FSR or connect with the Crumpit Woods option.

The 9-kilometer descent of the Ring Creek Rip will likely be a low-elevation classic for years to come. For a quick riding fix, you won't be disappointed.

APPROACH

From Horseshoe Bay, follow Highway 99 north toward Squamish. At the north end of the Stawamus Chief, about 1 kilometer north of the tourist lookout, turn right on Mamquam FSR. Park in the climber's gravel parking lot.

DISTANCE/ELEVATION LOG

0km	0m	From Highway 99, follow Mamquam FSR east along the north walls of Stawamus Chief.
4.5km	90m	From the wide open area at the junction with Stawamus FSR, start climbing east up Mamquam FSR.
9km	430m	Stay right (6-mile sign) down to Raffuse Creek.
15km	460m	Cross the Nine Mile Bridge.
15.1km	460m	Turn left onto the smaller side road and climb Lava Flow Hill.
16.5km	700m	Turn left in a clearing, 200m past the top of Lava Flow Hill. Prepare for an ultra-buffed singletrack that careens down a narrow corridor of overhanging alder.
21km	400m	Powerhouse Plunge to the left. See the option, below.

24km	290m	Trail reaches the Upper Ring Creek log crossing. A single big log. Be careful.
24.5km	290m	Join Garibaldi Park Road.
26.8km	92m	Ring Creek Falls Trail. Turn left and cross the Lower Ring Creek Footbridge (92m). Turn left onto the hydro line access road.
28.8km	90m	Pass the bottom of the technical Powerhouse Plunge. Cruise on. Cross the cement powerhouse bridge. Travel a short uphill and continue on the main road 1.5km back to Mamquam FSR and right back to the climber's parking lot in 4.5km, or turn a sharp right to moderate singletrack through Crumpit Woods.
35.5km	0m	Ride ends at the climber's parking lot.

OPTION: POWERHOUSE PLUNGE

| 21km | 400m | A sharp left will drop you into a dark forest with primo technical riding down to the Ring Creek Falls Trail (the hydro access road). This option is difficult technical riding, with steep drops, sharp cornering, and many obstacles. It also represents the most challenging section of the annual Test of Metal race. |

Ripping down from Lava Flow Hill on a perfect basalt base

OPTION: CRUMPIT WOODS

29.5km   90m   After crossing the cement powerhouse bridge, take a sharp right through a yellow gate that bars vehicle access to the Mamquam Powerhouse. The entrance to Crumpit Woods is at the top of a short hill. The riding here is in lush second-growth forest and is moderately technical with many entertaining obstacles. After about 3 kilometers, a fire access road will lead south to Mamquam FSR.

Duct Tape

This is the recreationalist's answer to, "Damn, it broke! So how do I fix it?" Duct tape, in combo with bailing wire, zip ties, or sticks, gives you unlimited ways to fix almost anything, even broken frames. After a friend's frame broke at the top-tube headset junction, a combination of the above got him 100 kilometers back to civilization. Obviously, with this intense a break, you won't be jumping too many logs on the return trip. Wrap a meter around the top tube before you set out.

4 POWERSMART

Loop trip: 20 to 25km
Duration: 3 to 4 hours
Elevation gain: 1,000m
High point: 960m

Season: April to October
Terrain: GG50%, ST50%
Rating: Difficult
Map: 92-G/11

There's nothing like manicured singletrack. This trail was created with the help of B.C. Hydro and some very dedicated local riders. This exciting ride is sure to help rate Squamish as a first-class North American mountain biking destination.

Powersmart is technical, combining steep climbs with fun cruising. Overall, expect a descent of nearly 1,000 vertical meters with the promise of an additional few hundred meters if a higher proposed start, off the Elfin Lakes doubletrack, is permitted in the future by B.C. Parks. If the full descent seems too numbing for your senses or if you don't want to cycle uphill to near the parking lot for Elfin Lakes, you can always enter the route midway.

Start the grind up Garibaldi Park Road, then turn onto Ring

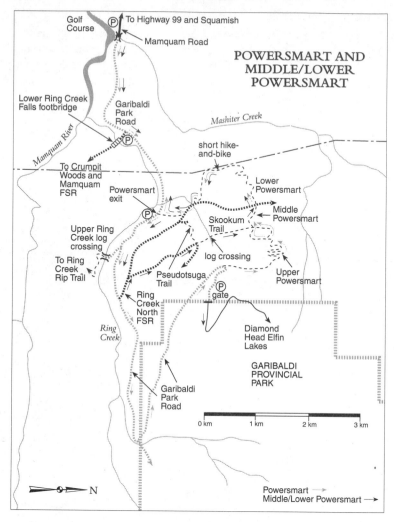

Creek North FSR to get to Middle and Lower Powersmart. Keep grinding right and uphill for another 10.6 kilometers and 860 vertical meters to reach a small skid road that takes you north to the technical Upper Powersmart in 1 additional kilometer.

Ring Creek North FSR will take you to Middle and Lower Powersmart. On your way you'll encounter two small options that are marked with varnished, very professional-looking signs. First is Pseudotsuga, then, 1 kilometer after a log crossing (after the turnoff for Lower Powersmart), the uphill Skookum Trail accesses Middle Powersmart.

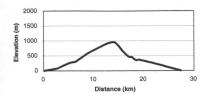

Lower Powersmart is super buffed and travels through a dense conifer forest. It's fast and fun with enough obstacles to make it interesting. Its 2-kilometer downhill run is split by a branch of Ring Creek FSR before re-entering the forest 50 meters north for the final blast to an old hydro access road. A traverse south with a 5-minute hike-and-bike will put you on the right track to carve some final turns before reaching Garibaldi Park Road.

This ride, coupled with the Ring Creek Rip, gives a sense of the excellent quality of singletrack in Squamish. If your time is limited, these technical rides are the ones to do.

APPROACH

Travel to north Squamish on Highway 99. Continue 5 kilometers past the townsite, cross the Mamquam River, and turn right on Mamquam Road. Follow this east until it changes to Garibaldi Park Road (gravel) at Mashiter Creek. Park here or at the Lower Ring Creek Falls footbridge (3km) or at the final exit of Powersmart at 4.7 kilometers.

Excellent singletrack trail construction on Powersmart

DISTANCE/ELEVATION LOG

0km	0m	Starting at the gravel road at Mashiter Creek, head east and start climbing up Garibaldi Park Road.
2.9km	92m	Stick to Garibaldi Park Road. Option: Junction with Lower Ring Creek Falls Footbridge. Possible parking. Links here to Crumpit Woods and Mamquam FSR.
4.7km	220m	Stay on Garibaldi Park Road. Final exit of Powersmart to the left. Possible parking.
5.9km	290m	Stay on Garibaldi Park Road. Option: Junction with Upper Ring Creek Falls log crossing. Access to the top of Powerhouse. Plunge on the Ring Creek Rip trail. Big dip in the road here.
6.5km	320m	Ring Creek North FSR on the left. Possible parking.
9.5km	650m	Road enters Garibaldi Park.
13.6km	960m	Turn left on a rough road where Garibaldi Provincial Park Road turns a sharp right.
14.6km	900m	Singletrack of Upper Powersmart turns left and drops steeply.
16.1km	600m	Junction with Skookum Trail. Right retains difficulty, left is easier.
17.1km	460m	Keep right.
17.6km	460m	Turn right and head down Lower Powersmart on excellent moderate-to-easy singletrack. Left heads to Ring Creek North FSR.
19km	380m	Junction with a lower branch of Ring Creek FSR. Turn right and ride 50m, then turn left down Lower Powersmart and go to the hydro lines. Turn left and hike-and-bike for about 10 minutes to rejoin the logging road, then turn right after a creek crossing to join Garibaldi Park Road.

OPTION: MIDDLE/LOWER POWERSMART

6.5km	320m	Turn left onto Ring Creek North FSR from Garibaldi Park Road.
8.9km	460m	Keep right at the Pseudotsuga Trail sign. Pseudotsuga is difficult and short.
9km	450m	Steep descent to a creek. Cross on a log and continue on.
9.9km	460m	Turn left for Lower Powersmart. Turn right up Skookum for Middle Powersmart access.
10.9km	600m	At the top of Skookum, turn left for the more difficult riding of Middle Powersmart.

5 ELFIN LAKES

Round trip: 23km
Duration: 3 hours
Elevation gain: 850m
High point: 1,660m

Season: July to October
Terrain: DT100%
Rating: Easy
Map: 92-G/11

Easy access and the high alpine environment make this a classic ride. Few rides put you in such exceptional terrain so quickly. While mountain bikes are not permitted on many park trails, this part of Garibaldi Provincial Park does permit them. Feel fortunate to be allowed in this special area and don't abuse your right of passage.

The route is an old road once used to access the old Diamond Head Lodge, now a part of history. What remains is a jeep road that is still used by B.C. Parks to supply the ranger station at Elfin Lakes, and a generally good track—with some loose rock and muddy areas after rain—for riding.

The route is completely surrounded by mountains: the Tantalus Range to the west, Mount Garibaldi and Diamond Head to the north,

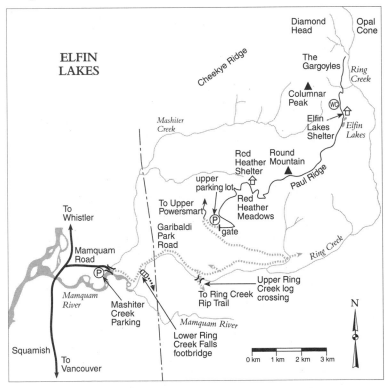

ELFIN
LAKES

Diamond Head
Opal Cone

Cheekye Ridge

The Gargoyles
Ring Creek

Columnar Peak

WC

Mashiter Creek

Elfin Lakes Shelter
Elfin Lakes

Red Heather Shelter
Round Mountain

upper parking lot
Paul Ridge

To Upper Powersmart
Red Heather Meadows

To Whistler
Garibaldi Park Road
gate

Mamquam Road
Ring Creek

Mamquam River
Mashiter Creek Parking

Upper Ring Creek log crossing
To Ring Creek Rip Trail

N

Mamquam River

Squamish
Lower Ring Creek Falls footbridge

To Vancouver

0 km   1 km   2 km   3 km

View of Mounts Atwell and Garibaldi from above Elfin Lakes

Mount Mamquam to the east. All have glaciers that cascade to treeline.

A gentle descent to Elfin Lakes provides superb riding around granite outcrops, past stunted subalpine fir, and through meadows of flowering heather. Eventually, the 11.5-kilometer doubletrack ends at the shelter and ranger outpost at the lakes. Campsites in the area make the trip suitable for an overnighter. Deeper in the park bikes are banned, but many hiking options exist.

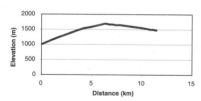

The best riding starts after the snow melts in July and continues into the fall. Be respectful of hikers and remember, your actions speak for the rest of us. Enjoy this special place.

APPROACH

Travel to Squamish north on Highway 99. Continue 5 kilometers past the townsite, cross the Mamquam River, and at the third set of lights turn right onto Mamquam Road. Follow signs 16 kilometers to the Diamond Head parking lot at 1,000 meters. If you wish to ride this 1,000-meter grunt to the parking lot, park at Mashiter Creek. Refer to Powersmart for the breakdown.

DISTANCE/ELEVATION LOG

0km	1,000m	Leave the upper parking lot, pass the gate, and start grinding up to Paul Ridge.
3.5km	1,450m	Red Heather Meadows and shelter.
6km	1,660m	Paul Ridge high point.
11.5km	1,470m	Descent to Elfin Lakes shelter and ranger outpost.

6 ALICE LAKE PROVINCIAL PARK

Loop trip:	Variable	Season:	September 15 to November;
Duration:	2-plus hours		February to April
Elevation gain:	50m to 150m	Terrain:	Mostly singletrack
High point:	400m	Rating:	Easy
		Map:	92-G/14

Trails in Alice Lake Provincial Park provide the rider with many out-and-back and loop options. The riding here is pleasant, short, and rewarding, especially because of its quiet, contemplative nature. Take a

Fall cruising near Edith Lake in Alice Lake Provincial Park

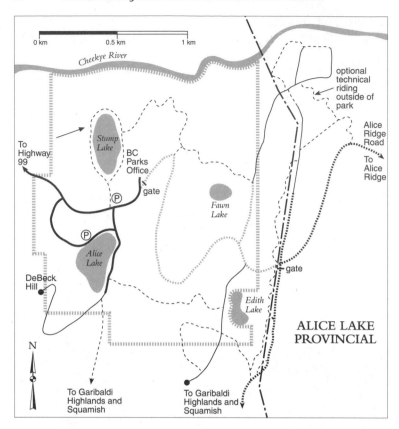

moment and immerse yourself in the Waldenesque surroundings. On a cool Saturday in March, I counted less than twenty people in this 400-hectare park, including fishermen and picnickers.

The Four Lakes Trail is the park's best offering. The riding suits the novice to a T and can be done in an easy morning. Trails loop

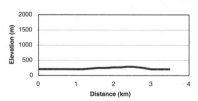

around and connect Alice, Fawn, Edith, and Stump Lakes with a great view from the top of 400-meter DeBeck Hill. The trails are well marked with signposts to help you get oriented. The riding undulates through stands of second growth cedar, spruce, and white pine. The decaying understory is carpeted with moss, making the forest floor look as if it has been covered in light green velvet.

Mountain bike access to the Alice Lake Provincial Park area is seasonal, with May 1 to September 15 off limits to any cycling. For longer rides of varying technical difficulty, an extensive network exists outside the park. Access through the park is on gravel road that starts 100 meters south of the park headquarters and runs to powerlines outside the eastern park boundaries.

APPROACH

Ten kilometers north of the Squamish townsite, turn right off Highway 99 at the entrance to Alice Lake Provincial Park. Drive up to the parking lot at either Stump Lake or the North Beach.

DISTANCE/ELEVATION LOG

0km	200m	At the Stump Lake parking area, head north.
1km	200m	Go right for Fawn Lake.
2.5km	300m	Turn right for Edith Lake. Option for going out of the park: Go left for easy riding for 2.5km.
3km	200m	Cross Alice Ridge Road (gravel).
3.5km	200m	Reach Edith Lake. Turn right and reach Alice Lake after 1km.

7   BROHM RIDGE

Loop trip: 32km	Season: July to October
Duration: 4 to 5 hours	Terrain: RG85%, DT15%
Elevation gain: 1450m	Rating: Difficult
High point: 1,700m	Map: 92-G/14

Ride till you bonk, then ride some more. The trip in its purest form—from the bottom with no pushing—will tax technical riding abilities both up and downhill. If you're able to do this ride, you truly must be nuclear. A fitness obsession may well be required to drive you to the end. As with all hard work, though, it is replete with rewards. Not only do you top out at a 1,700-meter-plus alpine ridge, but the views are superb. And, of course, the 1,400-meter downhill will evaporate all the sweat you perspired on the way up.

The route follows old logging roads consistently eroded by winter rain and snowmelt. The result is a track of loose rocks varying from ball-bearing- to fist-size. The surface makes for a high technical-grade venture, thanks to the lack of traction and the skill required to ride over and around bouldery obstacles.

The natural history of this area is extremely volcanic. The ride ends

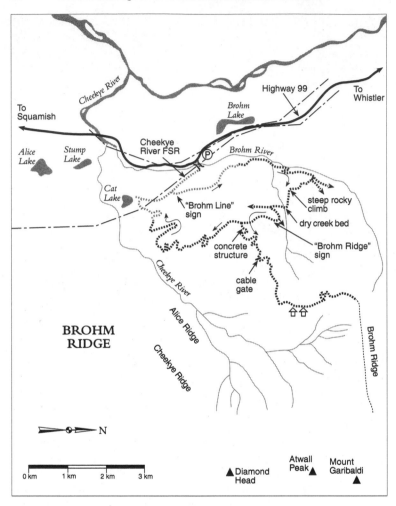

near the Garibaldi massif, part of the volcanic cordillera that is the Coast Range. Geologically, Brohm Ridge is considered very unstable. At the ridge top, look for fracture lines in the underlying soil layer—mostly ancient volcanic muds. In a future earthquake of substance, some geologists believe, a chunk of the ridge could slide to the valley bottom. If you're fortunate enough to be there when it happens, you may be in for the technical descent of a lifetime.

Despite its arduous nature, the Brohm ride is highly recommended. Aside from the hazards already mentioned, there are only a couple of wildlife considerations. In fall, because of the blueberries found along the route—great taste treats for bears and humans

The upper alpine on Brohm Ridge, with Mount Atwell behind ©Tomas Vrba

alike—you might want to carry bear spray. In summer, the flower blooms attract bees. If you're allergic to stings, be prepared.

A cool swim in Cat Lake near the end of the ride is your final bonus.

APPROACH

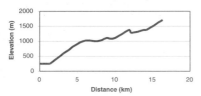

Fifteen kilometers north of the Squamish townsite, turn right off Highway 99 (about 1 kilometer south of Brohm Lake) onto Cheekye River FSR. This entrance is somewhat hidden by the highway embankment. Park on the roadside a short way in.

DISTANCE/ELEVATION LOG

0km	250m	Follow Cheekye River FSR through the tunnel of mature alders and cross the Brohm River.
1.3km	260m	Turn left at the BROHM LINE sign and start climbing.
5.3km	960m	Turn right onto a smaller, eroded road; 50m later turn right again and traverse southeast along the mountain. The climb is steep and rocky.
7.7km	1,000m	Stay right and cross a dry creek bed.
8.3km	1,040m	Turn left at the base of a small talus slope. Prepare for some technical boulder crawling.
8.8km	1,100m	Stay right at the BROHM RIDGE sign. Road levels and heads to the south.
10km	1,130m	Turn left onto the main road and start climbing. Pass a large concrete structure.
11.8km	1,370m	Pass by a hanging cable gate.
13.8km	1,380m	Stay left at the cabins and follow the narrow road up the ridge crest.
16.3km	1,700m	Ride ends at the ridge top. If you have energy to spare, follow the faint track up the ridge for another 2km. On the return trip, stay left at the fork a short distance past the concrete structure. This is an alternate descent back to the parking spot.

Packs for Riding

On longer trips, you may need both panniers and a pack for your extra gear. Choose a form-fitting pack, one compact enough that it will not ride up your back and push your helmet over your eyes. Good suspension with excellent padding is a must. Look for a lightweight pack with an internal frame of aluminum stays or with a moulded plastic insert; an external frame is too bulky and will set you off balance.

8 CHEAKAMUS CANYON

Loop trip: 37km
Round trip: 32km
Duration: 2.5 to 3.5 hours
Elevation gain: 300m
Season: April to November

Terrain: BT40%, RG20%, DT40%
High point: 400m
Rating: Moderate
Map: 92-G/14

Outstanding views of the Tantulus Range and Cheakamus Canyon make this a good, short, out-and-back foray. You have the option of returning to your vehicle by way of the pavement of Highway 99 or retracing your route.

To start the ride, in the words of Led Zeppelin, there are two paths you can go by. At 4 kilometers into the trip, taking a right turn gives uphill technical riding for another 4 kilometers to Highway 99 at Garibaldi Station. This option, the Starvation Lake Plunge, is also rumored to be a good place to test your new shocks. (Save it for the

Taking a break to look down into Cheakamus Canyon

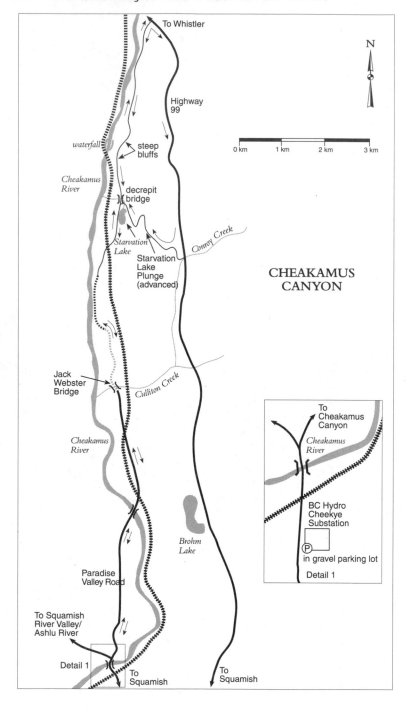

N

To Whistler

Highway
99

waterfall   steep
bluffs

*Cheakamus
River*

decrepit
bridge

*Starvation
Lake*

Starvation
Lake
Plunge
(advanced)

Conroy Creek

**CHEAKAMUS
CANYON**

0 km   1 km   2 km   3 km

Jack
Webster
Bridge

Culliton Creek

*Cheakamus
River*

*Brohm
Lake*

Paradise
Valley Road

To Squamish
River Valley/
Ashlu River

Detail 1

To
Squamish

To
Squamish

To
Cheakamus
Canyon

*Cheakamus
River*

BC Hydro
Cheekye
Substation

P
in gravel parking lot

Detail 1

return journey, exiting right off Highway 99 past Conroy Creek.) Keeping left, however, provides a slightly shorter, easier, and more scenic alternative, ending at the old blocked-off Tantalus viewpoint on Highway 99.

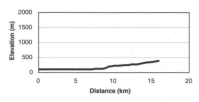

The ride is a short little bonus that also harbors other recreational opportunities. A swim at Starvation Lake is an option, especially if you're overheated and winded. But if you've pushed, ignored the ring of stars above your head, and continued on, you get full marks for being a hardcore. At the top, it's flat and views are good, and that makes it all worthwhile.

APPROACH

Ten kilometers north of the Squamish townsite, turn left onto Squamish Valley Road (opposite the Alice Lake Provincial Park entrance). After 3 kilometers, park in the vicinity of the B.C. Hydro Cheekye Substation. Cross the Cheakamus River and turn right (left goes to Squamish River Valley) up Paradise Valley and the Cheakamus Canyon.

DISTANCE/ELEVATION LOG

0km	100m	Cross the Cheakamus River. Keep right, onto Paradise Valley Road.
3.4km	110m	Cross railway tracks.
4.4km	110m	Head north on new road that parallels the railway tracks and powerlines.
8.5km	130m	Cross the Jack Webster Bridge and continue north under the powerlines on the main gravel road. After 1.8km the road narrows and follows the bank of the Cheakamus River. Get pumped for a series of steep and chunky climbs.
12km	250m	Cross the railway tracks.
12.5km	270m	South end of Starvation Lake. The outflow of the lake can flow down the trail during rainy periods; expect some boulder-hopping and wet feet.
12.7km	270m	North end of Starvation Lake. Continue north on the main trail, crossing a decrepit bridge over a small creek. The track starts to traverse along the steep bluffs above the Cheakamus River. Spectacular!
16.0km	400m	Trail ends at a blocked-off viewpoint on Highway 99.

OPTION: STARVATION LAKE PLUNGE

From the north end of Starvation Lake, climb the severely washed-out road that leads to Highway 99. This is a steep, challenging, lung-busting climb. From Highway 99 it makes a steep, fast route to the lake, which allows for an optional return loop.

9 SQUAMISH AND ELAHO RIVER VALLEYS

Round trip: 20km to 60km	Season: February to November
Duration: 3 to 8 hours	Terrain: GG100%
Elevation gain: 800m	Rating: Easy
High point: 800m	Maps: 92-J/3, 92-J/4

Few people know the wild terrain northwest of Squamish, an area scoured by glaciers and saturated with all that nature has to offer. Vast floodplains, narrow canyons, waterfalls, cliffs, hoarfrosted peaks, and endless snowfields give a stimulating introduction to Coast Range topography. The Squamish, Elaho, and Ashlu Rivers flow through it all.

The mountain biking is easy, fun, and all on logging roads. It's also all out-and-back riding. The Elaho and Ashlu are the roads less traveled; the Squamish is the most hectic. During midweek you'll likely encounter only logging trucks. All-season use is possible, but fall, winter, and spring are the best.

The Squamish mainline is well-graded and wide, and follows the vast floodplain of the Squamish River. It's hard to believe that during the spring freshet, all of this area can be inundated. The Squamish, although glacial in origin, swells as each tributary river and creek—including the Ashlu, Elaho, and Mamquam—joins in the journey south.

This ride can be divided into three segments. The first travels 20 kilometers from Cheekye to the first bridge over the Squamish River (where the road continues into the Ashlu Valley). The second travels 26 kilometers to the second bridge of the Squamish (and into the Elaho drainage). From here, the mainline continues right to the upper Squamish. Easy riding ends here. Roads into the headwater area steadily gain elevation for at least 20 more kilometers—still scenic, but the pedaling is harder.

The area deserves at least a weekend's worth of exploration. Sandy flats on the outwash plain provide a wealth of camping spots, especially when other campsites in the Sea to Sky corridor are full. December and January are the best months to view the record numbers of eagles

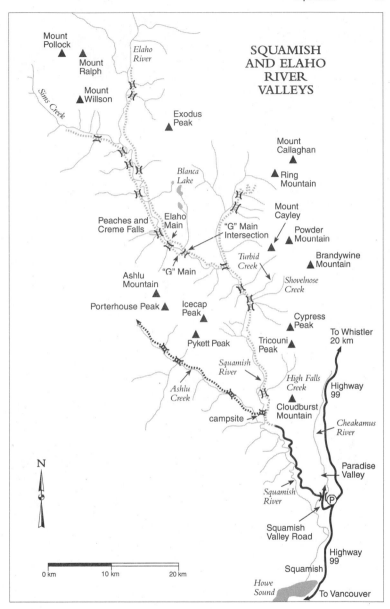

SQUAMISH
AND ELAHO
RIVER
VALLEYS

Mount Pollock
Mount Ralph
Mount Willson
Elaho River
Exodus Peak
Sims Creek
Mount Callaghan
Ring Mountain
Blanca Lake
Mount Cayley
Peaches and Creme Falls
Elaho Main
"G" Main Intersection
Powder Mountain
Brandywine Mountain
Turbid Creek
Ashlu Mountain
"G" Main
Shovelnose Creek
Porterhouse Peak
Icecap Peak
Cypress Peak
To Whistler 20 km
Pykett Peak
Tricouni Peak
Squamish River
High Falls Creek
Highway 99
Ashlu Creek
Cloudburst Mountain
Cheakamus River
campsite
Paradise Valley
N
Squamish River
Squamish Valley Road
Highway 99
0 km   10 km   20 km
Squamish
Howe Sound
To Vancouver

that come to feast on spawned-out salmon. Thick moss-covered cotton-woods and lichen-draped conifers give a moist, raincoast feel. Along the way, various side valleys present exploration opportunities—the best being the volcanic Vulcan's Thumb–Mount Cayley area, near the Elaho Valley junction.

Vulcan's Thumb stands sentinel over a rider near Turbid Creek ©Laszlo/Namu

At the second crossing of the Squamish River, keep left to soon enter the scenic Elaho Canyon. In the spring the standing waves on the river are amazing. After venturing through the canyon, the road enters the Elaho Valley proper. The riding extends 36 kilometers into the upper Elaho. Tremendous old-growth forest contributes to the dramatic feel of the original biosphere of the region. The tributary valley of the Clendenning is slated for protection as part of the Randy Stoltmann Wilderness. The Sims Creek area and the upper Elaho are slated for more road-building and logging. The riding is easy out-and-back and the scenery beautiful. Even a drive into the area to spend time exploring will not disappoint. It's truly wild, so discover the area while it's still intact. The valley is relatively low in elevation and so is snow-free for most of the winter. Some side roads are worth exploring. The "G" Main, 12 kilometers from the second bridge, leads to some great waterfalls.

APPROACH

Ten kilometers north of the Squamish townsite on Highway 99, turn left onto Squamish Valley Road (opposite the Alice Lake Provincial Park entrance). After 3 kilometers, park in the vicinity of the B.C. Hydro Cheekye Substation. After crossing the Cheakamus River, continue left on Squamish Valley Road. (Right goes to Paradise Valley and the Cheakamus Canyon.) If you wish to shorten your day, drive on and park at any point. The road turns to gravel 16 kilometers from the Cheakamus River Bridge.

SQUAMISH RIVER VALLEY
DISTANCE/ELEVATION LOG

0km	40m	After crossing the Cheakamus River Bridge, fork left up Squamish Valley Road.
16km	40m	End of blacktop.
20km	70m	Ashlu Valley junction.
46km	150m	Elaho Valley fork. Keep right for the upper Squamish Valley.
60km	800m	End of Upper Squamish Valley Road.

ELAHO RIVER VALLEY
DISTANCE/ELEVATION LOG

0km	150m	Start at the second crossing of the Squamish River, 46km beyond Cheekye.
3km	200m	Enter the Elaho Canyon.
12km	350m	Valley opens up at this point (Elaho Valley continues right). "G" Main intersects from the left. Option: Continue on "G" Main for Peaches and Creme Falls: outstanding (16km/450m). "G" Main continues for 40km up Sims Creek Valley.
36km	800m	Elaho Main ends.

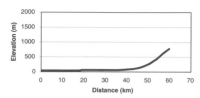

Squamish River Valley

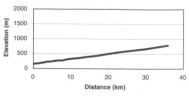

Elaho River Valley

OPTION: THE ASHLU VALLEY

At 20 kilometers, where the first bridge spans the Squamish River, turn left and cross the wide outwash plain. Within 2 kilometers is a campsite at the bottom of the Ashlu Canyon. Easy out-and-back riding follows this wilderness tendril for 60-plus kilometers until it degenerates into four-by-four road for the remainder.

Snow riding in the Ashlu Valley

WHISTLER/PEMBERTON

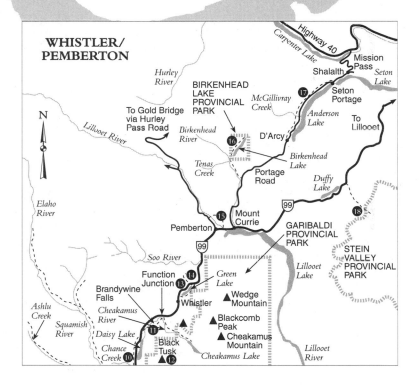

**WHISTLER/
PEMBERTON**

N

Hurley
River

BIRKENHEAD
LAKE
PROVINCIAL
PARK

McGillivray
Creek

Highway 40

Carpenter Lake

Mission
Pass

Shalalth

Seton
Lake

Seton
Portage

To Gold Bridge
via Hurley
Pass Road

17

Anderson
Lake

To
Lillooet

Lillooet River

Birkenhead
River

16

D'Arcy

Tenas
Creek

Portage
Road

Birkenhead
Lake

Duffy
Lake

Elaho
River

15

Mount
Currie

99

Pemberton

GARIBALDI
PROVINCIAL
PARK

18

99

Soo River

STEIN
VALLEY
PROVINCIAL
PARK

Function
Junction

14

Green
Lake

Lillooet
Lake

Brandywine
Falls

13

Ashlu
Creek

Cheakamus
River

Whistler

▲ Wedge
Mountain

Squamish
River

Daisy Lake

11

▲ Blackcomb
Peak

Chance
Creek

10

Black
Tusk

▲ Cheakamus
Mountain

▲

12

Cheakamus Lake

Lillooet
River

*T*wo hours north of Vancouver, the resort community of Whistler lies between the coast mountains at the summit of the Sea to Sky corridor. At an altitude of roughly 700 meters, winter is long and the skiing is outstanding. Mountain biking has become very popular and developed, in part because of local biking organizations and the annual Cheakamus Challenge bike race.

Pemberton, 33 kilometers farther north and 500 meters lower, is surrounded by peaceful farms. With the high mountain backdrop, this valley could easily be mistaken for Switzerland. Typical of British Columbia, though, the terrain is rough-hewn and lacks Switzerland's softness of landscape that centuries of habitation bring. When exploring the Pemberton area, it becomes quickly apparent that the area is less traveled. Major population centers are farther away and so are the crowds. Be prepared to be more self-sufficient.

Intersecting the wide Pemberton Valley are three tributary accesses to points beyond. Birkenhead Valley leads to Anderson Lake via the old Douglas Trail to Shalalth in 50 kilometers. The Duffey Lake Road (Highway 99) takes the high upland route over Cayoosh Pass to Lillooet in 98 kilometers, and the Hurley Pass Road to the northwest leads to the southern Chilcotin in 80 kilometers. Pemberton is a gateway hub to adventure.

Both Whistler and Pemberton offer rides that range from valley cruises to steep climbs to alpine destinations. Trips included in this book are a cross-section of mountain biking trails that give a good representative feel for the whole Whistler/Pemberton region. Most are half-day-plus excursions that will take you to the high alpine and hidden lakes, give great single- and doubletrack, show interesting geological and natural features, and whet your appetite for more.

Expect mountain weather to be changeable. Whistler is at the high point of the Sea to Sky corridor and tends to be influenced by marine weather. Pemberton is slightly drier, with the surrounding mountains stealing a portion of the moisture that travels in from the ocean.

The popularity of the Whistler area forces an even more rigid observance of trail etiquette. Many of the trails have hiker traffic, so be considerate. Despite the close proximity to this growing resort municipality, trails yield a wilderness flavor. By avoiding high-volume periods you can enjoy all the uninterrupted solitude that nature has to offer.

10 CHANCE CREEK TO FUNCTION JUNCTION

Loop or round trip: 40km	Season: April to November
Duration: 3 hours	Terrain: BT25%, GR15%, DT55%, ST5%
Elevation gain: 500m	Rating: Easy
High point: 700m	Map: 92-J/4

If the car smells like road trip and you're just itching for a ride to purge your system before heading back to the city, this short segment of the Sea to Sky Trail will do fine. Ride it either as a short, one-hour out-and-back from Chance Creek to Pinecrest Estates, or as a contiguous part of the Sea to Sky Trail connecting Brandywine Falls to Function Junction just south of Whistler.

Much of the southern part of the Sea to Sky Trail forms the race course of the annual Cheakamus Challenge mountain bike race. Chance Creek to Function Junction represents the 20-kilometer mid-section of the race, where the terrain flattens and gives riders a break before dramatically steepening again.

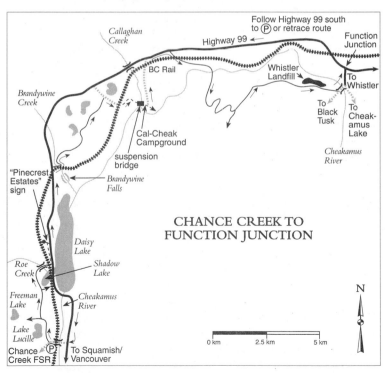

Splashing down in the basaltic tarns north of Brandywine Falls

Whether you choose to ride the trail in its entirety or in pieces, it is fun, with a mix of singletrack, doubletrack, gravel road, and some highway. The terrain is well-traveled but super-interesting because of

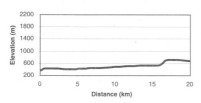

its geology. Be prepared to ride over a landscape of lava flows that have been scoured by the passage of time and ice. Glaciers gouged the dips now filled with water. In fall, these tarns become interconnected to form a series of great rideable puddles. Note the scarring on the otherwise smooth surface of the lava, caused by ice-borne rocks. The riding after Brandywine Falls gives a hint of what you might find in Moab—slickrock. When the lava cooled, it created basaltic columns. Octagonal and polygonal shapes may remind you of interlocking paving stones. The rolling terrain makes for speedy riding; just be sure to watch for hikers.

Singletrack along Callaghan Creek and a suspension bridge add interesting variety. The remaining 5.5 kilometers to Function Junction follow primitive powerline access roads linked with a bit of singletrack. Who knows? Maybe you'll want to come back and ride the Cheakamus Challenge.

APPROACH

From Squamish, drive 31 kilometers north on Highway 99 and turn left onto Chance Creek FSR. Cross the Cheakamus River and the B.C. Rail tracks, and park. From Whistler, drive south 29 kilometers on Highway 99 and turn right onto Chance Creek FSR and park.

DISTANCE/ELEVATION LOG

0km	370m	Chance Creek junction with Highway 99.
0.2km	370m	Keep right after crossing the Cheakamus River. Ride a moderately steep hill.
0.5km	435m	Keep right at the top of the hill and follow the wide main trail.
2.3km	430m	Southwest finger of Daisy Lake (also known as Shadow Lake). Turn left to pass the lake on the west. Scenic singletrack.
4.2km	410m	Bridge over Roe Creek; may be in disrepair.
5.5km	420m	Pinecrest Estates. Head north on Highway 99 toward Brandywine Falls.
10.6km	500m	Brandywine Provincial Park. Cross Brandywine Creek, turn left, and grunt up a short hill. (Turn right for a view of the falls.)
13.9km	530m	Turn right onto a gravel road and keep right to the railway tracks.
14.5km	530m	Cross the railway tracks (road ends) and turn left onto singletrack. Cross the Callaghan Creek suspension bridge. Pass through the Cal-Cheak Campground and turn left on the wide gravel road that heads back to Highway 99.
16km	550m	Turn right and ride up the highway for about 400m until you can take a right and cross the railway tracks through a gate. Head north on a wide trail, down to the Cheakamus River. Cross the river and climb to the top of the hill (700m) and keep left. Reach the Whistler Landfill (watch for possible black bears in summer), turn left, and follow the gravel road to blacktop and Function Junction.
20km	670m	Function Junction. Complete the loop via Highway 99 or retrace the route.

11 CHEAKAMUS LAKE

Round trip: 15km to 29km
Loop trip: 18km
Duration: 4 hours
Elevation gain: 280m
High point: 950m

Season: March to November
Terrain: GG45%, ST55%
Rating: Easy
Map: 92-J/2

Rolling, buffed, and moderately technical singletrack characterize this out-and-back ride. This adventure is a surprise gem worth discovering.

Start by either cycling or driving the Eastside Main access road east of Function Junction. The 7-kilometer jaunt to the Cheakamus Lake parking lot is most of the elevation gain (230 meters) for the

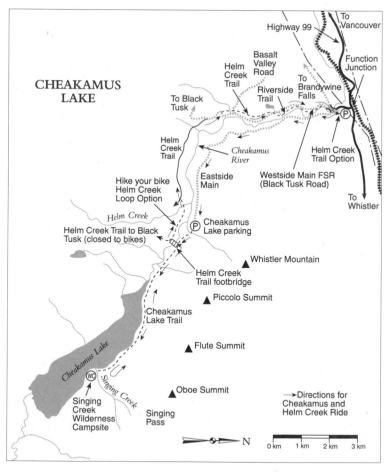

day. As you leave the remnant clearcuts and demonstration forests, enter Garibaldi Provincial Park. The park was established in 1927 and fortunately escaped the logging that scoured the surrounding areas in later years. Be prepared to see old-growth cedar and an open, mossy understory.

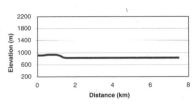

From the parking lot, travel a buffed track 3 kilometers to the Cheakamus River outflow at the west end of the lake. A 50-meter climb is negligible but is enough to give a dynamite descending spin to the lake. Hikers and walkers frequent the area, especially on summer weekends. Always yield on this multi-use trail or the privilege of riding here will soon disappear. This is the only trail other than the Elfin Lakes trail that is legal to ride on in the park.

Past the west end of Cheakamus Lake, the next 3.5 kilometers of trail is technical, with exposed roots, rocky drops, and wooden bridges. The difficulty increases when the terrain is wet. The less-adept rider may want to hike-and-bike some sections. Cross avalanche paths that give open views to the lake's milky waters against a backdrop of the Cheakamus Glacier and the 2,675-meter Castle Towers at the southeast end of the lake.

Near the Singing Creek Wilderness Campsite, Cheakamus Lake

Wilderness campsites at the west end of the lake and at Singing Creek give an overnight option. Adventurous and skilled riders might consider a night ride during the off-season. The Cheakamus Lake trail provides some extremely good singletrack that is sure to put a smile on your face.

APPROACH

Drive Highway 99 to Whistler. Eight kilometers south of the Whistler townsite, turn left at Function Junction. Possible parking here. Consider parking here if you want to make a loop via Helm Creek Trail. Turn left on Eastside Main in 500 meters and then travel 7 kilometers, gaining 200 meters in elevation to the Cheakamus Lake parking lot.

DISTANCE/ELEVATION LOG

0km	900m	Cheakamus Lake parking lot.
1.5km	830m	Helm Creek Trail footbridge.
3km	830m	West end of Cheakamus Lake. End of easy singletrack.
7.5km	830m	Singing Creek and wilderness campsite.

OPTION: HELM CREEK TRAIL

Cross the Cheakamus on the footbridge 1.5 kilometers from the parking lot. Travel west and hike your bike for 20 minutes (difficult) to join a kilometer of moderately technical singletrack. Join easy doubletrack to connect with Westside Main FSR (Black Tusk Road). Be attentive; in just over a kilometer, easy singletrack diverges left, paralleling the road. Follow this as it crosses Basalt Valley Road until the trail joins again with Westside Main. Cross and follow the easy singletrack of the Riverside Trail back to Function Junction for an 18-kilometer loop.

12 BLACK TUSK

Round trip:	32km	Season:	July to October
Duration:	6 to 8 hours	Terrain:	GG30%, RG70%
Elevation gain:	1,330m	Rating:	Difficult
High point:	2,000m	Map:	92-J/2

Hearty riders with a penchant for training and natural beauty will love this out-and-back pedal. The microwave tower near the 2,315-meter volcanic plug of the Black Tusk is your cycling destination. The quiet resolve that must be put forth to climb 1,300 meters over

The Black Tusk is a twenty-minute hike from the microwave tower

16 kilometers of rough road has its rewards, for the alpine views are stunning. Of all the rides in the Whistler area, no other gives such a spectacular panorama.

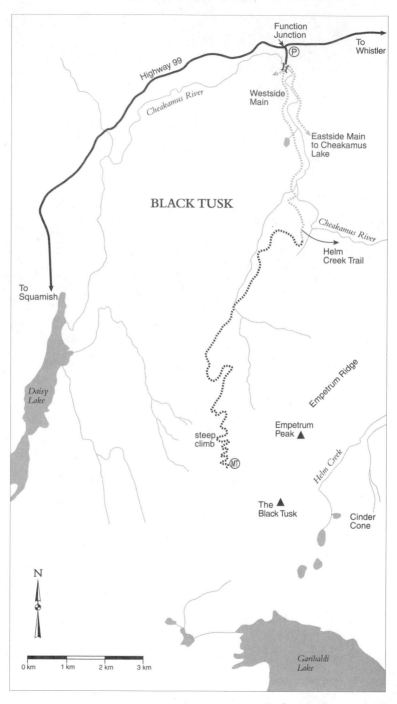

The ride starts out mellow. Cross the Cheakamus River and continue left on Westside Main. Warm up on the first 5 kilometers along the river in preparation for the initial switchbacks. The elevation gain makes for the first real sweat of the trip. Soon a mid-level plateau has you humming along in mid-ring rhythm. En route you'll find plenty of streams to slake the thirst you've worked up. The easy pace in this section allows you to conserve energy for the rest of the climb.

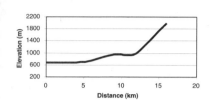

Stoke up on carbs, psych yourself up, and torque on. Cruise higher and higher until the forest thins and gives way to alpine meadow. The last kilometer of gnarly road involves technical uphill travel over fist- and noggin-size volcanic debris to the microwave tower. Collapse here and let the clouds cover you. If you still have energy, ditch your bike and hike on to the Black Tusk. Look at Tantalus Range etching the skyline to the west. On the way back, be sure to stop once in a while to cool the rims and shake out your forearms from the bumpy road.

Despite this ride's arduous nature, it is extremely worthwhile. If you're training for an endurance marathon like the Eco-Challenge, this burly ride has the added feature of increasing your cardiovascular pathways to help cope with the rigors of a multi-day event. For further abuse, carry a pack full of rocks.

APPROACH

Drive Highway 99 to Whistler. Eight kilometers south of the Whistler townsite, turn left and park at Function Junction.

DISTANCE/ELEVATION LOG

0km	670m	From the parking lot, ride down Westside Main, crossing the Cheakamus River. Continue left on Westside Main. Right goes to the landfill, Brandywine Falls, and Chance Creek.
5km	700m	Cycle along Westside Main and turn uphill.
9km	950m	Road plateaus.
12km	950m	Prepare for the final assault: a huge hill. Hork and heave through the many switchbacks.
16km	2,000m	You made it. Microwave tower. Enjoy the views and then the descent.

13 GREEN LAKE LOOP

Loop trip:	21km	Season:	April to November
Duration:	3 hours	Terrain:	BT45%, DT50%, ST5%; Thrill Me
Elevation gain:	300m		option: BT15%, DT50%, ST35%
High point:	800m	Rating:	Moderate; Thrill Me option, Difficult
		Map:	92-J/2

This Whistler loop is a classic, especially when combined with the technical singletrack of Thrill Me Kill Me, the optional route at the end of this write-up. You'll still feel the buzz of excitement a week later. From Meadow Park, start the Green Lake Loop by heading north

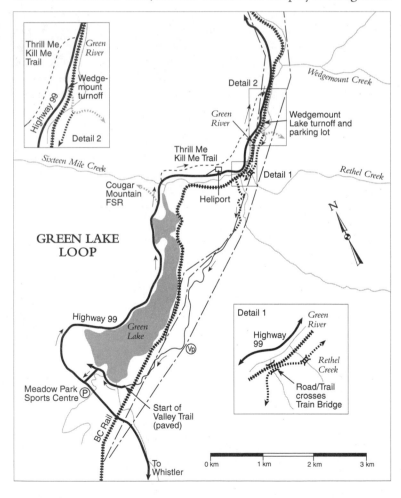

On the viewpoint overlooking the glacial waters of Green Lake

on paved trail and blacktop to the Wedgemount Lake turnoff. This makes up the first half and easiest part of the loop.

The last part of the loop follows a rough road that traverses the bluffs above Green Lake for 9 kilometers. The beginning may cause a bit of confusion, but if you stay right, cross the creek, and follow the railway tracks before heading left into the bush, you can't go wrong. This moderate track undulates, giving great views of the surrounding mountains and the glacially floured lake. Expect some rather chunky downhill through tunnels of alder before descending to Meadow Park on the south shore of the lake.

If you choose to ride the Thrill, start just north of the Cougar Mountain FSR. This will eliminate 7 paved kilometers before rejoining the road just north of the Wedgemount Lake turnoff. You'll have to backtrack on Highway 99 for about a kilometer to connect with the remainder of the route. Thrill Me Kill Me is characterized by drops off rocks, roots, speedy cruising, fall-line slab riding, and small creek crossings. You have to be on your game to reap the full enjoyment this singletrack deviation offers. If you're not, practice and be content for the time being to ride the road that makes up the easier first half of the loop.

APPROACH

From Whistler Village, drive 4.5 kilometers north on Highway 99 to the Meadow Park Sports Centre and park. If you want to cycle from the village, park in the huge day-use area on the east side of Lorimer Road. Travel to Meadow Park via the obvious Valley Trail. This adds an extra 9 kilometers to the overall trip.

DISTANCE/ELEVATION LOG

0km	640m	From Meadow Park, follow Highway 99 north. Turn right on blacktop or paved trail.
4.6km	640m	Cougar Mountain FSR.
4.8km	640m	Thrill Me Kill Me option starts to the left.
12km	640m	Turn left at the Wedgemount Lake turnoff and parking area; cross a bridge and bear right.
15km	640m	Cross a creek to the railway tracks and follow the trail to a washed-out area.
15.5km	640m	Follow railway tracks and exit to a small trail on the left. Arrive at the top of the hill and then head south on primitive road.
18.3km	738m	Top of another short hill. Mature second growth timber here.
19.5km	800m	View of Green Lake.
21km	640m	End of the hard stuff. Continue 1.8km along the valley trail to the vehicle.

OPTION: THRILL ME KILL ME

Start this excellent technical singletrack about 200 meters north of Cougar Mountain FSR, north off Highway 99.

0km	640m	Turn left off Highway 99 for singletrack.
1.4km	683m	Heliport on the right.
6.2km	660m	End of the trail at Highway 99. Head south 1.2km to the Wedgemount turnoff and parking area to continue the Green Lake Loop.

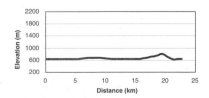

Green Lake Loop

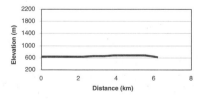

Thrill Me Kill Me

14 COUGAR MOUNTAIN/ANCIENT CEDAR GROVE

Round trip:	16km	Season:	April to November
Duration:	2 to 3 hours	Terrain:	GG25%, DT50%, ST25%
Elevation gain:	600m	Rating:	Easy
High point:	1,250m	Map:	92-J/2

If you want to escape the urban mountain culture of Whistler, do this out-and-back ride. This cedar grove is like an outdoor museum that gives you an idea of what forests in the area looked like pre-1925. There are few trees like these left in British Columbia, and virtually none left in the Sea to Sky corridor. Take time to look at the 800-year-old cedars and consider that when they were seedlings, the Crusades were scouring Europe.

Start this 2.5-hour ride near the end of Green Lake, 9 kilometers north of Whistler. Grind up Cougar Mountain FSR, staying right at all forks. At 4 kilometers the road steepens, then changes into rough

A few of the many ancient cedars that once grew in the Sea to Sky Corridor

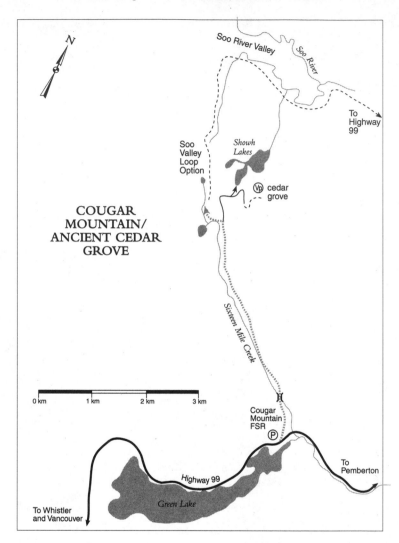

road. One kilometer farther a washed-out skid road marks the beginning of the 3-kilometer trail. Cycle on, gently gaining elevation until a 50-meter hill demands that you hike-and-bike to easier, more ridable terrain. Viewpoints here let you gaze over the clear-cuts to Showh Lakes and peaks to the west.

Soon, after bumping along over a few gnarly root and rock sections, a bridge crossing will have you at the intersection of the short cedar grove loop. Either walk your bike or lock it as you explore on foot, for

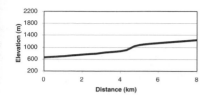

it's important not to damage the root systems of these magnificent trees. On weekends expect to see hikers. Be ethical and dismount.

Despite the short length of this out-and-back trip, the natural attributes make it a very worthwhile ride. It may also cause you to ponder the contrast of this grove's stately beauty and the consequences of clear-cut logging.

APPROACH

From Whistler Village, drive Highway 99 north. In 9 kilometers, near the end of Green Lake, turn left onto Cougar Mountain FSR and park.

DISTANCE/ELEVATION LOG

0km	650m	Highway 99.
4km	860m	Turn right. Left goes into Soo River Valley.
5km	1,070m	Turn right. Continue along the rough four-by-four road and gain elevation to the grove.
8km	1,250m	The cedar grove. Big old-growth cedar.

OPTION: SOO VALLEY LOOP

On the return trip, rejoin the main road at the 4-kilometer mark. Turn right and climb until a long descent leads down into the logged-out moonscape of Soo River Valley. En route, compare with the ancient cedars. Keep right on the valley floor and return to Highway 99. About 20 kilometers in all.

Pedal Creaking

This annoying sound can drive you nuts. It can be one of three things. The aluminum cranks may have worn, causing play against the steel axle. If so, try tightening the 14mm bolt behind the plastic cap that covers the bolt on the crank. The cranks will probably need replacing soon.

Your bottom bracket may be crying for lubrication. The simple answer? Add grease.

The pedals may be toasted. Keep in mind that if they do not rotate true, knee problems can develop. Often, neglected pedals need to be lubed, too. Always replace the dust caps or you'll eventually have to replace the pedals.

15 LILLOOET RIVER LOOP

Loop trip:	24km	Season:	May to November
Round trip:	20km	Terrain:	BT10%, GR45%, ST45%
Duration:	3 hours	Rating:	Moderate; Overnight Sensation
Elevation gain:	610m		option, Difficult
High point:	790m	Map:	92-J/10

You won't be disappointed with this quality, cool, scenic loop, which is the perfect introduction to Pemberton singletrack. Kudos go to valley locals who had a hand in linking a combination of old roads with singletrack to produce this 24-kilometer ride.

Several options should satisfy riders of all abilities. The first section of easy riding along the Lillooet River can be approached directly from the center of the Pemberton townsite in 2 kilometers via Poplar and Urdal Roads to the B.C. Rail bridge. The bridge has a walkway so you won't have to jump into the Lillooet River if you happen to be caught by a train. From here a super 1-kilometer, twisting connector trail puts you on the river trail proper.

The best novice access is by the Glider Highway, which is really a small local gravel road. Approach this via Highway 99, 3 kilometers east of the Petro-Canada gas station. Make a left turn onto the Old Pemberton Farm Road by the obvious log house. After 1 kilometer, turn left onto Glider Highway at the T intersection by the gravel quarry. This gives 4-plus kilometers of graded gravel and doubletrack riding, eliminating the bridge crossing before launching into the easy riverside singletrack.

Riders of all abilities will have a hoot howling through the riverside singletrack. A mix of cottonwood and cedar overhang the trail and bluffy sections provide expansive views of the farms across the river. A washout section ends the river trail.

Riders with more gusto may want to continue into the switchbacks of the old logging track that is the Mackenzie Basin Road. The 500-meter grunt can either be cycled or pushed. A short rest at the summit will put you in a better mood to approach the stellar singletrack that lurks in the bush ahead. The road continues east, but just before it gets super-steep, note the small spur that diverges left. Here the technical Overnight Sensation makes its devious way over terraces and bluffs, dropping more than 300 meters in 6 kilometers to the valley below. Less-experienced riders should probably stick to the road. Both routes end up in the same place, near the tracks at the gravel quarry, where the junction of Glider Highway and the Old

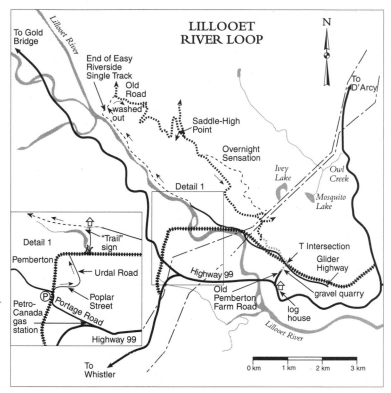

Pemberton Farm Road can take you back to the rail bridge.

In the bush above the gravel quarry, a network of trails descends from Mosquito Lake. Most of the rides are in the 1- to 2-kilometer range, dropping anywhere from 50 to 150 meters. True singletrack technocrats will have a field day here.

APPROACH

From the Pemberton townsite (parking lot of the Pemberton Hotel), cross Portage Road east to Poplar Street. Continue through a small subdivision for 0.5 kilometer and cross a narrow footbridge to Urdal Road. Head north on Urdal Road for 1.5 kilometers to the rail overpass. Follow the rail grade to the bridge crossing the Lillooet River. In 50 meters drop left. The 1.5-kilometer connector trail travels through a floodplain forested with cedar and cottonwood before meeting doubletrack from Glider Highway. Turn left on doubletrack to begin the riverside trail proper.

For those wanting to ride the Lillooet River as an out-and-back or a short loop back through Pemberton, the best approach starts 3

Great singletrack riding above the farms of the Pemberton Valley

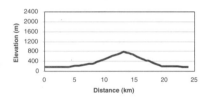

kilometers east of the Petro-Canada gas station, near the obvious log house. Turn left off Highway 99 onto the Old Pemberton Farm Road. After 1 kilometer, turn left at the gravel quarry to join Glider Highway. Follow Glider Highway west to cross the rail tracks, either to join the Urdal Road access or to continue on the riverside singletrack.

DISTANCE/ELEVATION LOG

0km	180m	Follow Urdal Road to its end.
2km	180m	Cross a rail bridge (via the walkway) over the Lillooet River. Turn left onto a connector trail.
3km	180m	Turn left and follow the road west through the forest. Glider Highway (gravel) joins here.
3.6km	180m	Stay right at the TRAIL sign. Ride past the last house and follow the trail west.
7.6km	305m	Stay right and climb up a short section of washed-out trail. At the top of the hill, the trail joins an old road.

8.2km	335m	Stay right and stick to the main road. Climb five switchbacks over the next 5km. Lung-busting and chunky. Hike-and-bike if you wish.
13km	790m	Stay left and ride through a small saddle (high point). Stay right as you descend.
14.1km	725m	Turn left for Overnight Sensation (see option, later). Right is easier and follows the old road down to the valley.
16.7km	450m	Stay right and limbo under the overhanging tree. Follow the trail to the road.
17km	440m	Stay right to rejoin the road.
17.2km	440m	Head left and downhill.
17.5km	410m	Stay right under the powerlines. Follow the main road down through switchbacks.
19.5km	190m	Cross the railway tracks and ride past the gravel quarry.
20.5km	190m	Turn right onto Highway 99, back to Pemberton.

OPTION: OVERNIGHT SENSATION

For technical and entertaining singletrack, take this 3-kilometer deviation at 14.1km/725m. Be prepared for great views, steep rocky riding, abrupt drops, and many obstacles. Check your brakes before you commit yourself.

16 BIRKENHEAD LAKE

Round trip: 38km   Season: May to November
Duration: 3 hours   Terrain: GG20%, RG40%, DT40%
Elevation gain: 300m   Rating: Easy
High point: 680m   Map: 92-G/10

If you want a perfect short break that will get rid of your road eyes and stretch your leg muscles, consider this ride. Both double and singletrack combine to give a pleasant non-technical out-and-back cruise. Gentle elevation gains and a cool, canopied forest also provide welcome respite on a hot day.

The area is storybook-like, especially in Birkenhead Lake Provincial Park. The forest is largely coniferous with an understory strewn with mossy boulders, decaying logs, and thickets of brilliant salmonberries. The odd squirrel may dart by carrying cones and chattering loudly at your presence. Yes, idyllic nature scenes—just be careful not to mush the little critters.

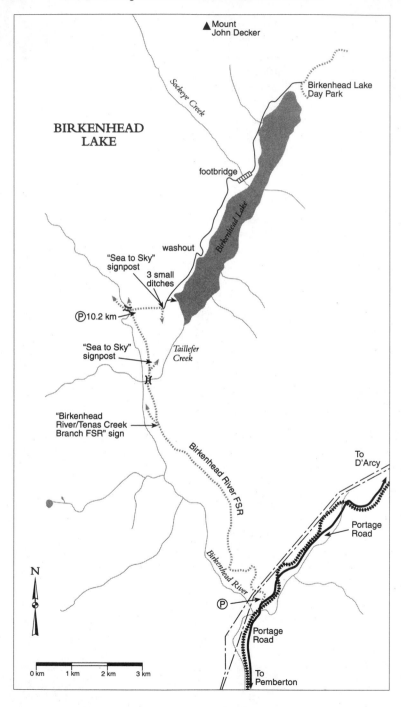

After the high point is reached 3 kilometers past the south end of the lake, expect a quick gentle descent with only a few rocky sections. The only difficulty is the Sockeye Creek crossing, which requires you to dismount, pop your bike on its rear wheel, and wheel it ahead of you over a single log. The bridge is handrailed on both sides to help out.

Reach the grassy picnic areas of the north end of Birkenhead Lake 8.7 kilometers from the road end. Swimming and the opportunity to watch beach life make this area a great place to rest. This path is part of the Squamish–D'Arcy Sea to Sky Trail.

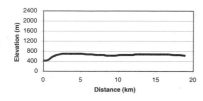

There are several options in the Birkenhead area. If your energy reserves are high and you like the backwater feel of the area, you might want to consider a longer loop. From the north end of Birkenhead Lake, take Blackwater FSR 17 kilometers down toward Highway 99. If your skills are up to it, consider a moderate 6-kilometer singletrack descent to D'Arcy, which starts about 2 kilometers beyond Blackwater Lake. Count on an additional 30 kilometers back to the trailhead for a total loop of 65-plus kilometers.

APPROACH

From Pemberton, drive 6 kilometers east on Highway 99 to the Mount Currie Indian village. Highway 99 continues on to Lillooet.

Sockeye Creek in full summer flood

Stay on the main road (Portage Road) through town and follow the signs to D'Arcy. After 25 kilometers, turn left onto Birkenhead River FSR. Cross over the railway tracks and park. The less energetic can drive on to the 10.2-kilometer mark and start there, thus eliminating over 20 kilometers.

DISTANCE/ELEVATION LOG

0km	430m	Continue on Birkenhead River FSR.
0.4km	430m	Turn left and start climbing up the gentle grade. Pass under the powerlines.
7.6km	640m	Stay right at the BIRKENHEAD RIVER/TENAS CREEK BRANCH FSR sign. Stick to the main road and gently descend and cross the Taillefer Creek.
8.9km	630m	Stay left at the SEA TO SKY signpost.
10.2km	650m	Take a right turn at the second bridge. Ride 30m up the road and then turn right onto a smaller side road. Cruise down through an open conifer forest. Parking option.
11.3km	640m	Go straight at the next SEA TO SKY signpost. Ride through three small ditches and join the wide track at the south end of Birkenhead Lake.
11.5km	640m	Stay left.
13.2km	670m	Take the bypass trail that switchbacks downhill to circumnavigate a large washout. It climbs and rejoins the main track.
14.5km	680m	High point.
16km	670m	Cross the narrow footbridge over Sockeye Creek.
18.9km	630m	Turn right into the parking lot at the Birkenhead Lake Day Park.

17 OLD DOUGLAS TRAIL

Round trip: 57km
Duration: Full day or overnight
Elevation gain: 1,300m
High point: 700m

Season: March to November
Terrain: RG100%
Rating: Moderate
Map: 92-J/9

Not only does this out-and-back trip give great views and a some-what hilly workout, it also provides an historic component. In 1858, Governor James Douglas proposed a unique deal to miners waiting to get to the Cariboo goldfields. Because it was too costly to build a road

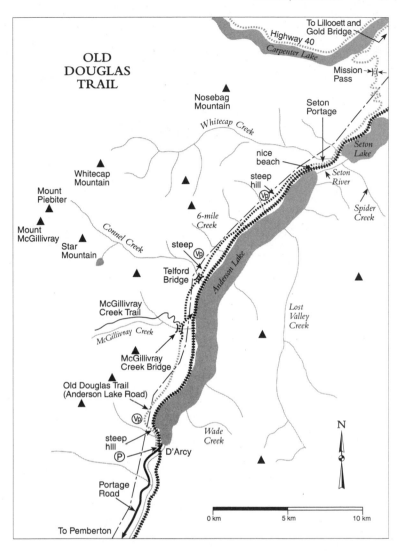

through the Fraser Canyon, he asked miners if they would build a trail connecting Harrison, Lillooet, Anderson, and Seton Lakes. They agreed to do it for room and board—a real political coup. Imagine trying this today! The trail fell into disuse in 1863 when the Cariboo Wagon Road along the Fraser was finally built. In the 1950s a four-by-four access road was built over roughly the same route to service the powerlines that run through the valley from the hydro complex at Seton Portage.

A high view of the almost 30-kilometer-long Anderson Lake

This ride travels the north shore of Anderson Lake. Views of the Cayoosh Range dominate the entire trip. The road is narrow and rough in some sections, with an overburden of loose rocks. Outside of a 400-meter grunt out of D'Arcy, the route undulates frequently in and out of small drainages that feed into Anderson Lake. Vehicles are the only other competition on this road. Because this route is not a real point-to-point destination time-saver, most traffic tends to be local or exploratory. People are friendly and willing to share stories about various exploits the area has to offer. This venture is scenic and provides a good tour, especially when snow bars the higher places.

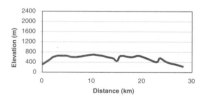

It's also possible to continue a further 73 kilometers from Seton Portage to Lillooet and retrace the route by rail. To do this means grinding 16 kilometers up the 1,200-meter Mission Pass Road before an exhilarating descent to Lillooet. There's more traffic here as well.

For those seeking exploratory adventure, another link is possible to the Bridge River Valley by traveling the old highline road east from the summit of Mission Ridge. The scenic, rough four-by-four road was blocked to vehicles by rock slides in the mid-1980s. The present condition is unknown.

APPROACH

Follow Highway 99 from Squamish north to Pemberton. Turn right at the Petro-Canada gas station and head toward Mount Currie Indian village, reached in 6 kilometers, then travel 40 kilometers on Portage Road to D'Arcy.

DISTANCE/ELEVATION LOG

0km	305m	Park in D'Arcy and backtrack 0.5km to a right turn that puts you onto the Old Douglas Trail (Anderson Lake Road).
10.2km	700m	McGillivray Creek Bridge.
13.7km	575m	Keep left; the road leads down to Anderson Lake (230m).
15km	450m	Telford Bridge and waterfall. Prepare for short, heinous climb.
15.5km	650m	Great viewpoint.
17.6km	600m	Six Mile Creek crossing.
19.5km	650m	Viewpoint across the lake to the Cayoosh Range.
22.8km	400m	Steep hill.
23.1km	575m	Viewpoint overlooking Seton and Anderson Lakes.
28.2km	230m	Seton Portage—time to turn around. Nice beach and possible camping.

18 BLOWDOWN PASS

Round trip: 31km
Duration: 4 hours
Elevation gain: 1,040m
High point: 2,200m

Season: July to October
Terrain: RG15%, DT85%
Rating: Moderate
Map: 92-J/8

Easy, accessible alpine and dynamite views make this trip outstanding. An old mining road goes right to the 2,200-meter summit and down the other side to the old Cottonwood Mine site.

As you enter Blowdown Creek Valley from Duffey Lake Road, look directly west into the sharp glaciated peaks of the Mount Joffre area. After gaining a bit of elevation in the first few kilometers, the road plateaus and subtly gains height. In the fall, red-berried mountain ash thickets mix with colorful groves of aspen. Soon the valley opens to reveal the granite cliffs of the upper Stein divide. Directly east, the meadowed ridge system of Gott Peak etches the skyline.

After about 9 kilometers, reach an obvious spur that is your conduit

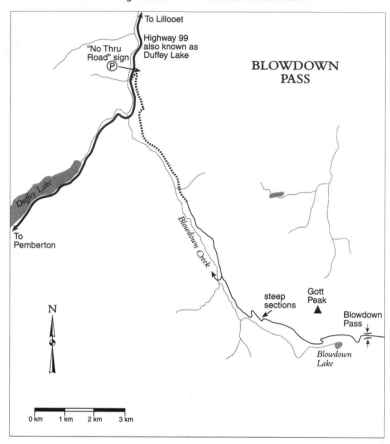

to Blowdown Pass. Another 6 kilometers and 700 vertical meters will have you top out with a hard-earned smile of success. The road is

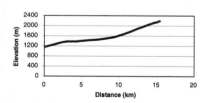

quite steep and loose with some washout sections. A fit rider with a light bike will probably be able to cycle most of this road. Non-nuclear riders will likely regard this section as a gut-wrench and may have to push once in a while; but look forward to the descent! You'll be on the valley bottom in minutes, picking the bugs out of your teeth.

If you have the energy, hiking and scrambling opportunities abound, and there's also a further venture 12-plus kilometers east to the old Cottonwood Creek Mine. The undulating ridge of Gott Peak presents excellent high alpine rambling with a chance of seeing goats. Fog and mist on inclement days may disorient you; be aware.

From the summit looking west, you'll notice the tantalizing waters of Blowdown Lake. On the way back (don't ride your bike across the fragile meadow), reward yourself with a cool dip and some good photos.

APPROACH

From the Mount Currie townsite east of Pemberton, travel east on Highway 99 (Duffey Lake Road) for 46.5 kilometers. Turn right toward the Blowdown Creek Valley and park. Ignore the NO THRU ROAD sign.

DISTANCE/ELEVATION LOG

0km	1,160m	Gain elevation up a small road.
2.5km	1,350m	Profuse fireweed in the fall. Valley begins to open.
5km	1,400m	Granitic peaks to the west. Ridge of Gott Peak (2,460 meters) to the east.
9.3km	1,538m	Stay left and follow doubletrack uphill. Fill waterbottles in the nearby creek.
13.5km	2,000m	Access to Blowdown Lake. *No riding here.* 500m elevation gain in the previous 4km. No woofing. Totally open alpine.
15.5km	2,200m	Summit of Blowdown Pass.

Great views from the 2,200-meter summit of Blowdown Pass

FRASER VALLEY

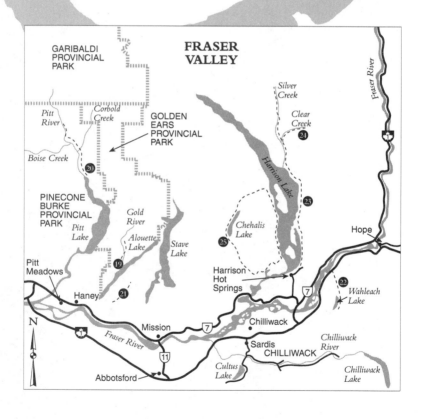

FRASER VALLEY

GARIBALDI
PROVINCIAL
PARK

Pitt
River

Corbold
Creek

GOLDEN
EARS
PROVINCIAL
PARK

Silver
Creek

Clear
Creek

24

Boise Creek

20

Harrison Lake

PINECONE
BURKE
PROVINCIAL
PARK

Gold
River

Pitt
Lake

Alouette
Lake

Stave
Lake

Chehalis
Lake

23

25

Hope

19

Harrison
Hot
Springs

Pitt
Meadows

Haney

21

7

22

Wahleach
Lake

N

1

Fraser River

Mission

7

Chilliwack

Fraser River

Sardis
CHILLIWACK

Chilliwack
River

11

Abbotsford

Cultus
Lake

Chilliwack
Lake

*T*his region contains an excellent cross-section of mountain-biking possibilities and the greatest concentration of riders. Networks of new and old logging roads traverse the region. Adventurous loops can also be linked, combining singletrack and logging roads. Exploration abounds with the scenic Coast Mountains as a backdrop. Lakes can be found along many routes or at destination's end. Rivers with peaceful pools will beckon a swim or the cast of a line.

The frenetic search for local singletrack in the past few years and a growing number of riders have conspired to cause overuse of some existing trails. The room for abuse and degradation of singletrack trails can be exacerbated by high traffic, especially in inclement conditions. New trails have been built—some of them unsanctioned and often substandard because of inexperienced builders. Once a ride is discovered and popularized, the track often cannot withstand the volume. For this reason, and because Vancouver's North Shore is already well known, we have chosen not to include riding in the Seymour, Cypress, and Grouse areas in this book. Most of those trails are overused. Support your local bike organizations for reconstructive efforts and maintenance.

The Blue Mountain Ridge area was initially developed for motocross activity and contains a wealth of exploratory and technical singletrack. For those of us who love the spills, chills, and challenges of singletrack, we have the moto-community to thank. To prevent these trails from falling victim to over-riding, work with user groups to connect and build a responsible network for mountain bike trail use and maintenance.

Note: Contact Cycling B.C. in Vancouver—John Wakefield, at (604) 737-3034—for education, advice, and support.

19 GOLDEN EARS CANYON

Round trip: 14km
Duration: 2 to 3 hours
Elevation gain: 160m
High point: 300m

Season: March to December
Terrain: DT65%, ST35%
Rating: Easy
Map: 92-G/8

West coast rain forest in its dark, fecund glory makes this a cool cycle on a hot day. Minimal elevation gain helps create a pleasant, out-and-back introductory ride. Some rooty sections provide challenge requiring the beginning rider to experiment with balance. Slippery when wet is the only cautionary note.

A forest floor in various stages of rot gives rise to a slimy biosphere, with fungus, fern, moss, and lichen eking out a sporific existence. Late in the day, you can almost feel a presence here when alone. There might be a possibility of a gnome or Sasquatch sighting. Cycle on before they carry you away.

The track starts as an old logging road with some corduroy sections still intact. Stumps from turn-of-the-century logging can be seen in the groves of devil's club. Slick bridges over small creeks call for

A bike takes a rest on the misty gravel beaches of Gold Creek ©Tomas Vrba

attention. The trail narrows and follows Gold Creek near deep pools and beside gravel beaches. The old-growth forest is no less than spectacular, with huge, bearded cedars arching skyward.

While the first 6 to 10 kilometers are easily managed by beginners, the trail becomes considerably rougher farther toward Hector Ferguson Lake. For the remaining 7-plus kilometers to the lake, masochists may wish to carry; others may hide their bike and hike. Watch for huge old growth and the odd hike-and-bike section.

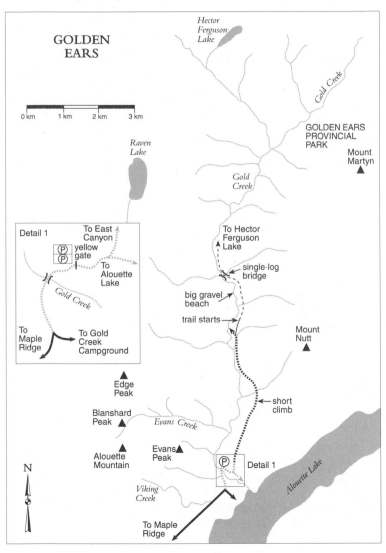

APPROACH

From Vancouver on Trans-Canada Highway 1, take exit 44 on the west side of the Port Mann Bridge and head north to Coquitlam on Highway 7. Cross the Pitt River Bridge (zero your odometer). Head east to the intersection with Dewdney Trunk Road in Pitt Meadows (6.5 kilometers east of the Pitt River Bridge). From this intersection, travel east 12 kilometers to 232nd Street in Maple Ridge. Turn left and follow the Golden Ears Provincial Park signs. Once in Golden Ears Provincial Park, head for the Gold Creek Day Area. The blacktop turns to gravel 20 kilometers from 232nd Street. A parking area here gives access to the trailhead, at a yellow gate.

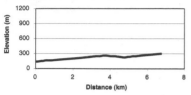

From points east, travel Trans-Canada Highway 1 to Abbotsford and take Sumas exit 92 north to Mission and head west to Haney. Watch for the Golden Ears Provincial Park signs.

DISTANCE/ELEVATION LOG

0km	140m	Ride around the yellow gate, which is there only to bar vehicles, and follow the old logging road through the forest.
0.3km	150m	Turn left and ride under the cool canopy of cedar, maple, and cottonwood trees. This road is easy going for most of its length.
4.7km	230m	Keep right.
5.2km	250m	Road ends and trail starts. Follow it along the riverbank and through the forest. Wide and smooth at the start, the trail gets more technical farther upstream. Roots and rocks are the main ingredients.
6km	280m	Excellent gravel beach. Good rest stop.
6.8km	300m	Cross a single-log bridge. The trail becomes very technical as it heads up the valley to Hector Ferguson Lake, reached in approximately 12km. Expert riders only beyond here.

Headset Bearings

Think about replacing these once a year and check the races while you're at it. To make them last longer, try stretching a 5-cm shank of innertube over the headset bearings for mud protection.

20 UPPER PITT RIVER

Round trip: 44km	Season: March to November
Duration: 3-plus hours	Terrain: GG90%, RG10%
Elevation gain: 250m	Rating: Easy
High point: 200m	Maps: 92-G/7, 92-G/10

Finding new places to ride is always exciting. Adventure starts as you pull away from the dock at Grant Narrows in Pitt Meadows. Your waterborne 15-kilometer journey north will give you an appreciation for the inaccessibility of the area. Steep granite walls shear into the water, giving a definite coastal-fjord feel. Closer to the destination, the lake waters turn a paler shade of blue-green, tempered by the glacial flow of the upper Pitt River. You could easily be in Toba, Bute, or Knight Inlets on the British Columbia coast, or even in northern Norway, by the remoteness of the area. In reality, you're less than an hour away from the third-largest city in Canada.

This area boasts six permanent residents and many bears. The attraction of the upper Pitt River is lots of wild land and few people. Logging still takes place on weekdays, but that will likely be over in a few years, when the allowable timber supply is exhausted.

On the bridge crossing the upper Pitt River

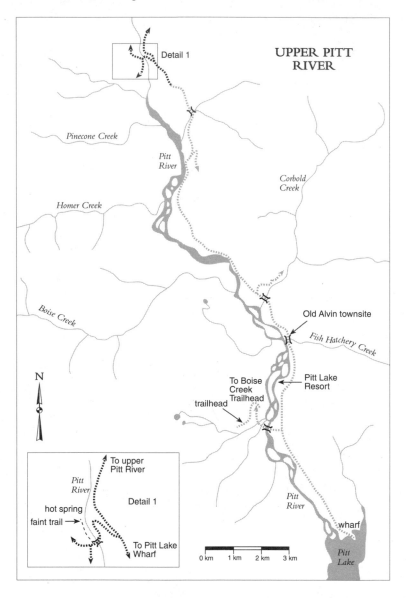

The upper Pitt offers several worthwhile out–and–back riding destinations. Two hours and 22 easy kilometers after docking, river hot springs will help soothe your muscles. The pools beneath the canyon walls stay a constant 40 degrees Celsius and are so close to the river that it's possible to cast into the current for elusive steelhead. Be careful not to fall in. The current is swift and cold, contrasting dramatically with the steaming hot spring.

Another gravel road provides access to the new Pinecone–Burke Provincial Park. A left turn 5 kilometers from the wharf provides access to the East Boise Trailhead. The ride covers 15 kilometers and gains 1,000 meters in elevation. At the trailhead an hour-long walk will put you in the heart of Cedar Spirit Grove. This special stand of old-growth western red cedar was the focal point behind the protection of the Boise Creek Valley.

Camping with amenities and possible vehicle support can be arranged through the Pitt Lake Resort. Other camping spots abound on the many gravel bars that line the river. If you desire an escape with some easy riding in some wild country, and want to go through the trouble of arranging boat transport, you will not be disappointed.

Note: Bears are in the vicinity. Make noise and carry spray.

APPROACH

Reach this area via Trans-Canada Highway 1 by taking exit 44 on the west side of the Port Mann Bridge. Follow Highway 7 north toward Coquitlam and the Pitt River Bridge. From Highway 7, turn left at the first set of lights, onto Dewdney Trunk Road, 1 kilometer east of the Pitt River Bridge. Stay on Dewdney Trunk Road for 6.5 kilometers and turn left on Neaves Road (208th Street). This becomes Rannie Road and travels north 18 kilometers to Grant Narrows at the south end of Pitt Lake. If you don't have access to a boat, you'll have to hire one to get to the north end of the lake. There are no direct boat rentals at Grant Narrows. For boat and camping information, call Dan or Lee Gerak at Pitt Lake Resort; phone or fax (604) 520-1796.

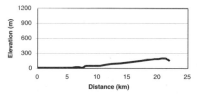

DISTANCE/ELEVATION LOG

0km	0m	Wharf at the mouth of the Pitt River.
5km	3m	Option: Turn left for the Boise East Trailhead. About 15km and 1,000m.
7km	3m	Pitt Lake Resort. Possible camping here.
8km	50m	Old Alvin townsite.
10km	50m	Corbold Creek.
21km	200m	Turn left and downhill toward the hot springs.
22km	150m	Cross upper Pitt River. Hot springs are 0.25km north, in the canyon.

21 BLUE MOUNTAIN RIDGE

Round trip:	23km	Season:	Year-round
Duration:	3-plus hours	Terrain:	RG100%
Elevation gain:	720m	Rating:	Moderate
High point:	1,020m	Map:	92-G/7

Blue Mountain is large and relatively complex. To increase your scope of the area, this out-and-back ridge ride will serve you well. Plenty of exploratory options will also entice you off the main track.

The ridge ride begins where the pastoral farms of McNutt Road in Maple Ridge yield to second-growth conifer forest on the southern flanks of Blue Mountain. The riding is moderately technical, following a worn and partially washed-out logging road. The first few kilometers are steep but then the road plateaus, working its way up into an old cutblock. By the time you've reached the end of the nearly 12-kilometer road, you'll have been entertained by over half a kilometer of short challenges. Granite ledges, boulders, and loose rock all combine to make the trip exciting. Viewpoints near the end of the road open to the surrounding peaks. As an added bonus, blueberries are profuse in season.

Cruising Blue Mountain singletrack at speed

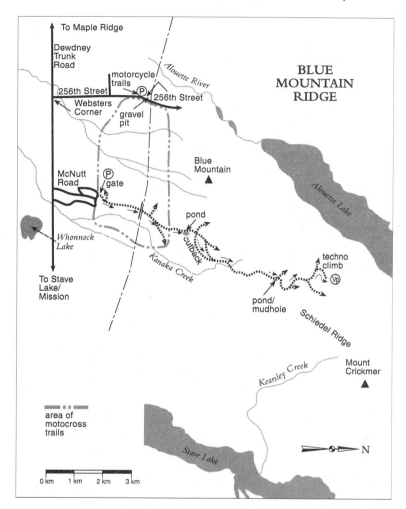

Once you're familiar with the area, you'll be able to link up with existing trail networks. Adventurous options may include a bushwhack/carry to connect east to the Kearsley Creek trail. The possibilities are endless and can occupy you for days. This area also has the reputation of being a good place to ride in the winter on snow compacted by various fossil-fuel-burning recreational vehicles.

APPROACH

From Vancouver on Trans-Canada Highway 1, take west exit 44 off the Port Mann Bridge north onto Highway 7 to Coquitlam. Head

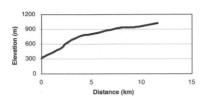

east on Highway 7 and zero the odometer at the Pitt River Bridge. At 6.5 kilometers, turn left on Dewdney Trunk Road in Pitt Meadows and follow it east through Haney. (For the Blue Mountain singletrack option, turn left at Websters Corner [256th Street] in 13 kilometers.) At 20.7 kilometers, turn left on McNutt Road. At 22.3 kilometers, turn left on Blue Mountain Crescent. At 22.5 kilometers, turn right on Blue Mountain FSR and park. Do not block the gate.

From points east, travel Highway 1 to Abbotsford, take Sumas exit 92 north to Mission, and head west to Haney. Dewdney Trunk Road can be reached from here.

DISTANCE/ELEVATION LOG

0km	300m	Pass the gate and ride up the road.
0.15km	340m	Stay right and enjoy easy cruising for 1km before climbing straight up the mountain via a steep, chunky climb.
2km	520m	Go straight.
2.3km	600m	Stay left and continue climbing.
3.8km	760m	Turn right and ride through the cutblock. The road levels as you reach the ridge.
4.9km	800m	Stay right.
8km	940m	Stay right after passing by a pond/mudhole.
8.9km	940m	Stay left.
9.2km	940m	Turn left. This branch climbs to the highest point and gives the best views.
10.3km	980m	Turn right. The last climb is the most challenging. A series of steep granite ledges with loose rocks will test any rider's technical ability.
11.6km	1,020m	Road ends at the ridge's high point. View the Golden Ears and Mount Robie Reid.

OPTION: BLUE MOUNTAIN SINGLETRACK

There are about one hundred singletrack trails on the lower flanks of Blue Mountain, 13 kilometers east of the Pitt River Bridge and 3.5 kilometers north of Websters Corner (256th Street). Park just before the powerlines. Explore and enjoy. Some trails may require a personal flotation device if it's wet, as some of the puddles and mudholes are quite deep.

22 WAHLEACH LAKE

Round trip:	25km	Season:	April to November
Duration:	3 to 5 hours	Terrain:	RG100%
Elevation gain:	625m	Rating:	Easy
High point:	650m	Map:	92-H/4

The out-and-back mountain biking in the Wahleach Lake area is perfect for beginners. This hidden area is worth the trouble if only for the northern views of the Cheam Range. Icefalls and spire-like peaks prompt you to get closer and tempt you to leave your bike and hike some of the alpine ridges.

In the early 1950s, Wahleach Lake was a serene, picturesque little tarn nestled beneath the towering peaks of the Cheam Range. In 1952 the surrounding shore was clear-cut and the lake became a reservoir, supplying water to a B.C. Hydro power station on the Trans-Canada Highway. Low water levels can turn the lake into a puddle, with waterlogged stumps dotting the shoreline.

The Cheam Range on a perfect, crisp fall day ©Lazslo/Namu

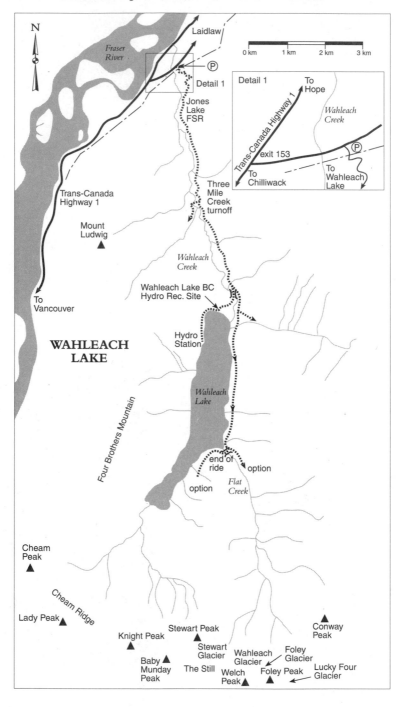

The first 6 of the 9 kilometers that it takes to climb the 625 meters to the lake are the steepest. Should you decide to ride rather than drive—persevere. The descent is a scream; do your best to keep in control. If you miss a turn, you may launch into space as some of the drops on Jones Lake FSR are unguarded and in excess of 200 meters. Traffic may also be present—a terrifying scenario, especially if you're without brakes.

Rough roads exist on both sides of the lake. The eastern road ventures toward Flat Creek in the south. Views are impressive and will have climber-types salivating over the quick access to excellent mountaineering possibilities. The westside road is short and ends at a small hydro station. Several old spur roads may also yield hidden riding gems. Consider taking a rod, for you may find an overlooked trout pool. A hydro recreation site at the south end of the lake has several campsites if you decide to stay overnight.

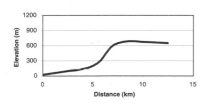

APPROACH

Turn off Trans-Canada Highway 1 at exit 153, about 15 kilometers west of Hope. After 1 kilometer, turn right onto Jones Lake FSR.

DISTANCE/ELEVATION LOG

0km	25m	Head right, uphill.
5km	200m	Three Mile Creek turnoff.
7.5km	650m	Side road forks right to B.C. Hydro Recreation Site and lake.
9km	650m	Reach Wahleach Lake.
12.5km	650m	End of lake. Option: Go right, gaining 250m in 3km. Stunning views. Go left for views from upper Flat Creek.

Grease All Threads

Before putting any bolt or nut on your bike, apply a little grease to its threads. This will allow you to torque the bolt down tighter, help prevent stripped threads, and prevent corrosion of the bolt/nut and the bike frame.

23 HARRISON LAKE EAST

Round trip:	88km	Season:	Year-round
Duration:	6 to 7 hours	Terrain:	GG100%
Elevation gain:	600-plus m	Rating:	Easy
High point:	360m	Maps:	92-H/5, 92-H/12

This out–and–back ride follows Harrison East FSR. Scenic attributes are reason enough for doing it, although it is also access for Clear Creek and the Silver River drainage. Its close proximity to Harrison Hot Springs means heavy summer weekend vehicular traffic. You must cope not only with drivers but with dust as well. Schedule this ride for the fall, winter, or mid–week summer when the area is not so hectic.

Harrison East FSR is well maintained and graded, with rock bluffs, waterfalls, and groves of old growth along the way. After about 10 kilometers, climb the only steep hill on the road to a viewpoint.

A Hans Rey technical riding move on a Harrison Lake pebble beach

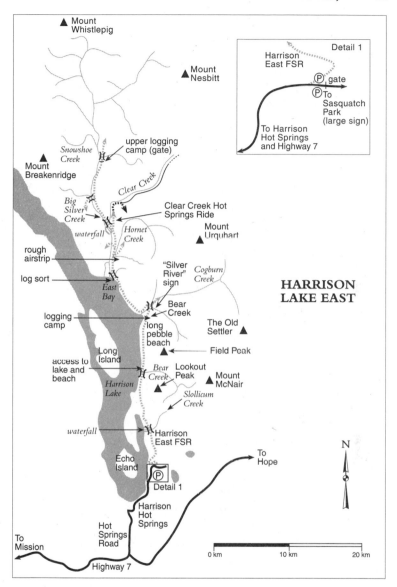

The sheer expanse of Harrison Lake makes you feel like a grain of sand on a big beach. The contrast between man and nature is striking. Views are liberated west to the Chehalis Range and Garibaldi Provincial Park.

A fast descent to the lake will deposit you on a fantastic pebble beach at about 20 kilometers. You may decide to call this the day's destination. Those who want to continue to Silver River—another 10-plus kilometers—will be rewarded by a peaceful riverine setting with camping possibilities.

APPROACH

Drive Highway 7 east to Harrison Hot Springs. Turn left on Hotsprings Road and travel 6 kilometers to Harrison Hot Springs townsite. Go through the main town (just before the beach at the south end of Harrison Lake) and turn right onto Lillooet Avenue (zero your odometer). Follow the SASQUATCH PARK signs. At 6 kilometers past Lillooet Avenue, turn right. At 7 kilometers, turn left on Harrison East FSR and park.

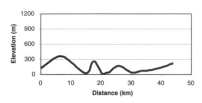

DISTANCE/ELEVATION LOG

0km	120m	Climb up the wide, buffed Harrison East FSR for several kilometers. It will level and then alternate short climbs with descents. Stick to the main road.
6.6km	360m	Pass a spectacular waterfall. Bask in the cooling spray.
14.5km	30m	Access to the beach and lake.
20.2km	30m	Stop at this long, narrow, pebble beach. Great views up and across Harrison Lake.
21.7km	40m	Pass the logging camp.
22.8km	80m	Cross the main road and turn left at the SILVER RIVER sign. Road narrows and crosses Talc Creek, and starts to climb.
30km	40m	Pass through a log sort. The road leaves Harrison Lake and turns northeast up the Silver River Valley.
32km	60m	Ride along a rough airstrip.
33km	70m	Stay left and stick to the main road.
33.5km	85m	Stay right.
35.2km	90m	Stay left. Clear Creek Hot Springs ride to the right.
41km	130m	Stay right and climb.
44km	230m	After following the Silver River, reach the upper logging camp. Report to the watchman if you want to proceed farther. A possible link may exist here to the Nahatlatch Valley and the Fraser River for those who might want to explore farther. Consult a topographic map.

24 CLEAR CREEK HOT SPRINGS

Round trip: 26km	Season: March to November
Duration: 3 to 4 hours	Terrain: RG65%, DT35%
Elevation gain: 610m	Rating: Difficult
High point: 700m	Map: 92-H/2

Environmentalists have identified this gorgeous creek valley and hot springs as a wilderness area deserving protection. For mountain bikers, the terrain gives a 26-kilometer out-and-back ride that includes a challenging washed-out section. Clear Creek Hot Springs is the destination—a soak will make you forget the uphill struggle that it took to get there. On the ascent, the route passes through small cutblocks interspersed with patches of standing Douglas fir. Across the valley, high

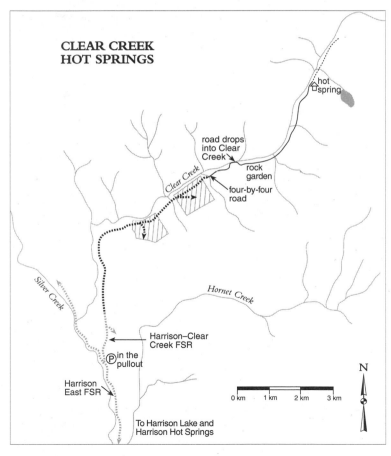

CLEAR CREEK
HOT SPRINGS

hot
spring

road drops
into Clear
Creek

Clear Creek

rock
garden

four-by-four
road

Silver Creek

Hornet Creek

Harrison–Clear
Creek FSR

in the
pullout

Harrison
East FSR

N

0 km   1 km   2 km   3 km

To Harrison Lake and
Harrison Hot Springs

Rock garden riding on a washed-out portion of the Clear Creek ride
©Tomas Vrba

peaks provide an impressive backdrop to a green mountainside dotted with bleached snags from a forest fire.

The road gains 500 meters in the first 8 kilometers before it presents any technical difficulty. The next 5 kilometers are a technical rider's dream. The old four-by-four road gains a further 250 meters, gradually degenerating into a track fraught with ledges and short drops. Remember, you can always hike-and-bike. The first kilometer is only a warm-up; the next 4 are worse— or better, if you enjoy a technical

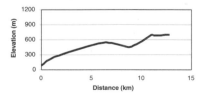

challenge. Get your forearms pumped and the granny gear primed, and give it a try.

The area can be quite popular on the weekends, with some attendant rowdiness. If you time it right, this worthwhile area can be surprisingly quiet.

APPROACH

Approach as you would for the Harrison Lake East ride. After 35.2 kilometers, on Harrison East FSR, park in the pullout at the beginning of Harrison–Clear Creek FSR.

DISTANCE/ELEVATION LOG

0km	90m	Turn right onto Harrison–Clear Creek FSR and start climbing.
1.3km	260m	Go straight and follow this easy road up the valley. The only challenges to be found are numerous deep waterbars and the occasional steep hill.
5.6km	520m	Stay left and cruise the lower road into the shady forest.
7km	550m	Stay left and follow the road into the cutblock.
8km	490m	Join up with the old four-by-four road. Immediately the travel becomes very technical. Follow the rough road up the Clear Creek Valley.
9km	460m	Descend to Clear Creek. Here the road drops into the creek and goes upstream for about 20m. The next 2km are fraught with rock gardens where the creek has run rampant. You may want to hike-and-bike.
12.8km	700m	Ride ends at the hot spring. If you are gung-ho, you can follow the overgrown road farther up the valley. Interesting topography and old growth trees.

Cartridge Bearings

Even sealed bearings need to be maintained. If you have cartridge bearings on your bike, a quick and easy way to extend their lifespan is to carefully pop the nylon seals (using a thin-bladed knife) and then pack grease into the races. Re-install the seals and wipe off any excess grease. This procedure should increase the bearings' life by 2 to 3 times. If you are a real grease monkey, you can clean the old grease out with solvent before re-packing the bearings.

25 CHEHALIS RIVER–HARRISON LAKE LOOP

Loop trip: 90km
Duration: 6 to 7 hours
Elevation gain: 1,000m
High point: 520m

Season: April to November
Terrain: GG95%, RG5%
Rating: Moderate
Maps: 92-H/5, G/8

Get stoked, shake the winter doldrums, and start thinking about riding. Here is the perfect excursion to start your spring training. Adventure and a good calorie-burn will help you get motivated for the rest of the season. Cross over the divide between the Chehalis and Harrison drainages and you'll experience a low-elevation loop ride available for early spring exploration.

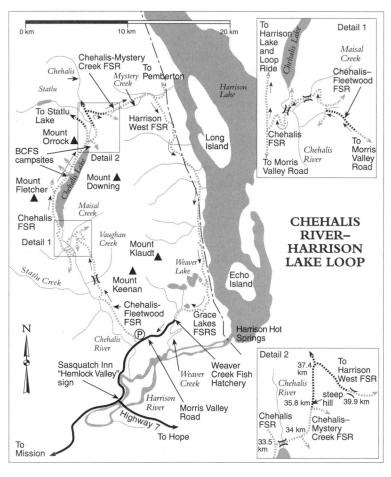

A calorie-replenishing pig-out and a rest beside Chehalis Lake ©Tomas Vrba

Head to the Hemlock Valley Ski area and cross the Chehalis River. At 0.5 kilometer, turn left onto Fleetwood FSR. Follow the road and at the first major fork, stay left for the Chehalis–Harrison loop. Follow the main road and cross first Maisal Creek and then the high bridge over the Chehalis River. At 19 kilometers, turn onto Chehalis–Fleetwood FSR and cruise north above Chehalis Lake. Continue past the Forest Service Recreation Site (FSRS), cross the river, and you'll be on Chehalis–Mystery Creek FSR. Keep climbing to a small pass at 520 meters for views of the Chehalis Lake and the mountains behind Statlu Lake. A 6-kilometer descent will take you to the Harrison West FSR and eventually to the valley bottom.

This loop is almost 90 kilometers long. Overall the climbs are minimal and many side roads give opportunity for further discovery. If you are too out of shape to do all 90 kilometers, think about breaking this ride over two days and camp at the recreation site at the north end of Chehalis Lake.

Note: There is active logging in this area. Riding is restricted to weekends and after 6:00 P.M. on weekdays.

APPROACH

From Vancouver, drive Highway 7 east to Mission, or Trans-Canada Highway 1 to Abbotsford and north to Mission via Sumas

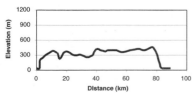

exit 92. From the first set of traffic lights at Wren Street, zero your odometer and continue east for 28.8 kilometers. Turn left onto Morris Valley Road (by Sasquatch Inn and the HEMLOCK VALLEY sign). At 35

kilometers, cross the single-lane bridge over the Chehalis River and park. In 0.5 kilometer, turn left at the start of Chehalis–Fleetwood FSR.

DISTANCE/ELEVATION LOG

0km	40m	Start up Chehalis–Fleetwood FSR. Stick to the main road.
9km	360m	Cross the bridge at Vaughn Creek.
13.2km	350m	Go right, cross through a tiny creek, and follow the level road.
13.7km	340m	Turn left onto the main logging road. Shift onto the big ring and enjoy the zip down to the Maisal Creek Bridge.
15.5km	200m	Stay left and cross the Chehalis River.
19.2km	380m	Make a sharp right onto Chehalis FSR. Stick to the main road and head north. Ignore all side roads.
33km	220m	Go straight. The right branch goes to a BCFS campsite at the north end of Chehalis Lake.
33.5km	280m	Turn right onto Chehalis–Mystery Creek FSR. Cross the Chehalis River. Hike option: For Statlu Lake, keep left for almost 2 kilometers, cross Statlu Creek, and turn left.
34km	290m	Stay left. Recent logging may have marginally altered the access.
35.8km	300m	Stay left and start climbing.
37.4km	300m	Stay right through the main switchback.
39.9km	520m	Stay left and ride over the unnamed pass. Take a breather and big-ring it down the gentle grade of Mystery Creek.
45.6km	360m	Turn right (uphill) onto Harrison West FSR. Follow this south, ignoring all side roads. Option: Turning left will take you to Lillooet Lake and Pemberton in about 120km.
82.8km	130m	Pass by Grace Lakes FSRS.
83.3km	40m	Join Morris Valley Road at the Weaver Creek Fish Hatchery. Follow the blacktop back to your vehicle (89km).

CHILLIWACK RIVER VALLEY

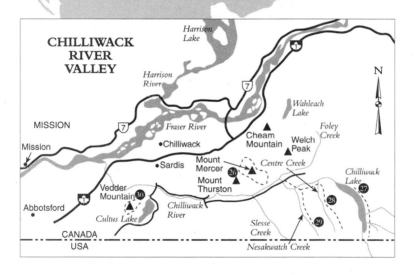

*T*he Chilliwack River Valley is composed of scenic, steep-walled peaks and a variety of smaller tributary drainages that spill into the Chilliwack River. Mountain biking here can be demanding at times but also rewarding—especially when you achieve your goal. Riding tends to be on logging roads that vary in condition from well-graded to semi-overgrown and partially washed-out. Challenges exist if you look for them.

A major portion of the existing singletrack in the Chilliwack River Valley has been developed by various motocross groups. The lower flanks of Mount Mercer contain a good collection of worthwhile low-elevation test pieces. We've included several as options; the rest of the exploration is up to you.

Chilliwack River tributary valleys, even though they have seen some logging, still give a wilderness feel and typify what you'd see in remote coastal British Columbia valleys. In your exploration, wildlife will enrich that experience. Once you struggle up the initial elevation of the hanging valleys, not only will the riding be easier, but the scenics will be outstanding.

The valley systems of the Chilliwack River have much to yield for mountain riders of all abilities. The mountain environment here dictates that you be prepared for every weather circumstance. As well, be aware that in recent years some local wayward youths have developed a penchant for miscreant behavior. Safeguard your possessions accordingly at the trailhead while you're out riding.

26 MOUNT THURSTON/MOUNT MERCER LOOP

Loop trip:	34km	Season:	June to November
Duration:	4 to 5 hours	Terrain:	RG100%
Elevation gain:	1,220m	Rating:	Moderate
High point:	1,570m	Map:	92-H/4

Of all the rides in the Chilliwack area, this one stands out for total coastal variety. The route has everything from waterbars to creeks, mud, gravel, and singletrack, old growth and clearcuts, perfect high mountain scenery, and, in autumn, mega blueberries. There's also the added attraction of it being a loop, with alpine high points of more than 1,600 meters.

The trip begins with a steep climb that continues for more than 4 kilometers before leveling out. For the next few kilometers the gain is more moderate before a climb to a divide that separates the Chilliwack River Valley from the upper Fraser Valley. Logging slash quickly gives way to open forest supported by undergrowth thick with Sitka mountain ash, false hellebore, thimbleberry, and blueberry. Follow this undulating ridge into old growth forest, where flowing streams of lichen pour from mossy branches. The cool shade here provides an excellent respite from the heat of the day.

The route descends to a saddle on the ridge before climbing to the ride's high point on the west side of Mount Mercer. This is a perfect lunch stop, with copious blueberries on which to pig out. Unrestrained excitement at finding such a profuse natural treat can easily result in purple lips, teeth, and fingers.

On top of Mount Mercer, consider a nap to digest the blueberries before attempting the dynamite downhill descent. From the ridge, blast at warp speed down the narrow road, sliding through switchbacks covered in loose gravel and through streams that create steam on hot rims.

Near the bottom of the 34-kilometer Mount Thurston/Mount Mercer Loop

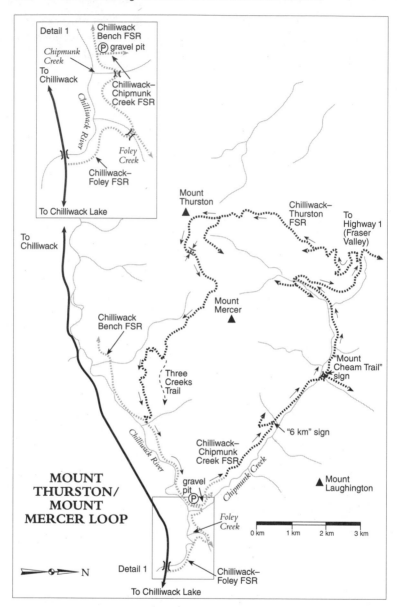

Take care in the descent; you wouldn't want to do a superman over the bars and ruin a perfect day.

The downhill soon ends, leading into the cool canopy of the Chilliwack Bench FSR. An easy 3.2-kilometer pedal along the pristine pooled waters of the Chilliwack River returns you to your vehicle.

APPROACH

From Vancouver, take Trans-Canada Highway 1 east to Chilliwack. Turn right at Cultus Lake–Sardis exit 119. Drive 5 kilometers south to Sardis and the metal truss bridge (zero your odometer) crossing the

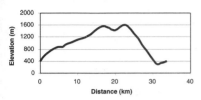

Chilliwack River. Turn left and head east up the Chilliwack River Valley. Cross the Chilliwack River at Tamihi Rapids (10km). At 27 kilometers, after crossing another bridge over the Chilliwack River, turn left onto Chilliwack–Foley FSR. At 29 kilometers, cross Foley Creek and turn left. At 31 kilometers, turn right onto Chilliwack–Chipmunk Creek FSR and park at the gravel pit.

DISTANCE/ELEVATION LOG

0km	400m	Climb up Chilliwack–Chipmunk Creek FSR.
4.3km	850m	Go straight at the tree with the 6 KM sign.
6.1km	870m	Cross Chipmunk Creek.
6.7km	940m	Stay left at the fork with the MOUNT CHEAM TRAIL sign. Road becomes level after a short hill.
10.3km	1,120m	Turn right and start climbing.
12.6km	1,230m	Turn left onto Chilliwack–Thurston FSR. Climb four switchbacks en route to the ridge crest.
16.1km	1,540m	Stay right and follow the smooth, narrow road along the ridge top. Travel through sections of standing forest and small cutblocks.
19.8km	1,420m	Stay right and climb up to the pass between Mount Thurston and Mount Mercer.
23.4km	1,570m	Cruise through the pass and alpine meadows. Get pumped for a brake-pad-melting descent to the bottom of the Chilliwack River Valley.
27.9km	930m	Option: Go left for Three Creeks Trail.
30.9km	320m	Turn left onto Chilliwack Bench FSR.
33.7km	400m	Parking area at the gravel pit.

OPTION: THREE CREEKS TRAIL

Another, more direct approach to the Three Creeks Trail and a network of short singletrack motocross trails can be accessed from the gravel pit. From the parking area at the gravel pit, follow Chilliwack Bench FSR right (west) for 2.8 kilometers to Chilliwack–Thurston FSR and turn right, riding 3 kilometers (930 meters) up to the entrance of the trail.

27 CHILLIWACK LAKE EASTSIDE ROAD

Round trip:	26km	Season:	March to November
Duration:	2-plus hours	Terrain:	RG100% (occasionally graded)
Elevation gain:	100m	Rating:	Easy
High point:	650m	Map:	92-H/4

A Friday night commute after a week of work in the stultifying city has you wasted. You pull in late at the Chilliwack Lake Provincial Park and crash. Picture a cool summer dawn that awakens your senses. For a ride before breakfast, you're in the perfect position for the perfect cycle.

For almost 13 kilometers the undulating gravel road follows the east shore of Chilliwack Lake. In the morning, the lake is serene with hardly a ripple. You might even see a canoe cutting the reflections that Mounts Lindeman, Webb, and MacDonald cast on the surface of the lake. It's the most peaceful time of day.

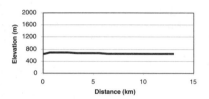

Sappers Park at the south end of the lake is the destination for this out-and-back ride. Sapper is a nickname of the Royal Engineers (Chilliwack Canadian Forces Base). The hardy military group had a camp here when they cut a swath through the forest that visually marks the border and the 49th parallel.

The Chilliwack Lake Eastside Road offers a quick ride for the cyclist who wants the perfect early morning escape. The road surface

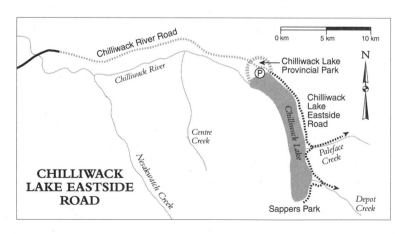

Looking out over the serene water of Chilliwack Lake

is rough but compact and occasionally graded, providing a relatively fast track. There is very little overall elevation gain en route. Paleface Creek at 8 kilometers and Depot Creek at 10 kilometers provide interesting out-and-back side trips.

APPROACH

From Vancouver, take Trans-Canada Highway 1 east to Chilliwack. Turn right at Cultus Lake–Sardis exit 119. Drive 5 kilometers south to Sardis and the metal truss bridge that crosses the Chilliwack River. Turn left and head east up the Chilliwack River Valley. After 40 kilometers, reach Chilliwack Lake Provincial Park at the north end of the lake.

DISTANCE/ELEVATION LOG

0km	650m	Start at the campsite entrance. Turn right.
1km	650m	Descend a small hill—the biggest on the whole trip.
8km	650m	Option: Go left for the Paleface Creek side trip.
10km	650m	Option: Go left for the Depot Creek side trip.
13km	650m	Sappers Park, at the south end of Chilliwack Lake.

28 CENTRE CREEK VALLEY

Round trip: 27km
Duration: 3-plus hours
Elevation gain: 640m
High point: 1,200m

Season: May to November
Terrain: GG25%, RG35%, DT40%
Rating: Easy
Map: 92-H/4

For coastal mountain scenery that is both accessible and beautiful, check out this somewhat challenging but very rewarding out-and-back ride. From the trailhead, the route follows a disused logging road that's in good four-wheel drive condition.

After a short, steep section the road plateaus, sweeping into a classic coastal hanging valley. Outstanding views abound, especially to the south, where the steep granite buttresses of Mount Rexford (2,330 meters) plummet to the valley floor.

The road continues south directly beneath the glacial cirque of

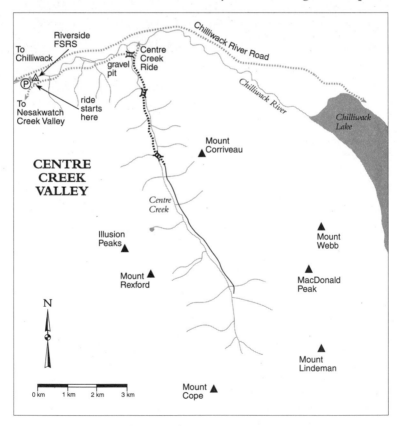

Riding upper Centre Creek in front of 2,310-meter Mount Lindeman

Mount Rexford to the United States border. In season, jewel-toned alpine flowers and citrine-yellow skunk cabbage enliven the meadows surrounding the creek headwaters.

Overall, the cycling is easy to moderate—a very rideable track, quite sandy with little mud. The Centre Creek Valley is a hidden gem, ideally suited for the intermediate rider or the novice with a bit of spirit.

APPROACH

From Vancouver, take Trans-Canada Highway 1 east to Chilliwack. Turn right at Cultus Lake–Sardis exit 119. Drive 5 kilometers south to Sardis and the metal truss bridge (zero your odometer). Turn left onto the Chilliwack River Road and head east up the Chilliwack River Valley.

Elevation (m)

Distance (km)

Travel 10 kilometers and cross the Chilliwack River at Tamihi Rapids. Pass by Slesse Creek at 21 kilometers and turn right at the 31-kilometer mark; cross the Chilliwack River and park near the Riverside Forest Service Recreation Site (FSRS).

DISTANCE/ELEVATION LOG

0km   560m   From the parking area, turn left for Centre Creek.

3.5km   560m   Pass a gravel pit and gain 100m to the lowest Centre Creek Bridge. Turn right.

5km   800m   Cross a second bridge over Centre Creek.

8km   1,000m   Stay on the main road.

8.5km   1,000m   Bridge.

9.5km   1,100m   Pass an old, steep logging road.

13.5km   1,200m   Road ends 2km north of the American border.

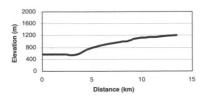

29 NESAKWATCH CREEK VALLEY

Round trip: 27km
Duration: 2 to 3 hours
Elevation gain: 440m
High point: 1,000m

Season: May to November
Terrain: GG40%, RG60%
Rating: Easy
Map: 92-H/4

Big views of big mountains make the Nesakwatch a de rigueur ride. Although a bit steep, the out-and-back trip is within the range of most novice riders. Starting in the valley bottom at 560 meters amid a mixed canopy of alder and maple, the ride tops out more than 13 kilometers later at about 1,000 meters. It's a fresh, clean, cool beginning to austere mountain views. Plan this ride for a clear day.

At about 3 kilometers, the Pierce/MacFarlane cirque is visible to the west, with a waterfall that plunges dramatically to the valley bottom. Mount Pierce is the peak to the north. At 5 kilometers, the valley begins to open up. A short climb through some recent cutblocks brings dramatic views of Mount Rexford to the east and Slesse Mountain to the west. At 8 kilometers, the valley opens even wider and the riding plateaus. In fall the subalpine shrubs burst into deep shades of red and orange, so bring the camera. The road continues in somewhat rough form to near the valley head and the United States border. If you have extra energy, explore the area south of Slesse for more views, but

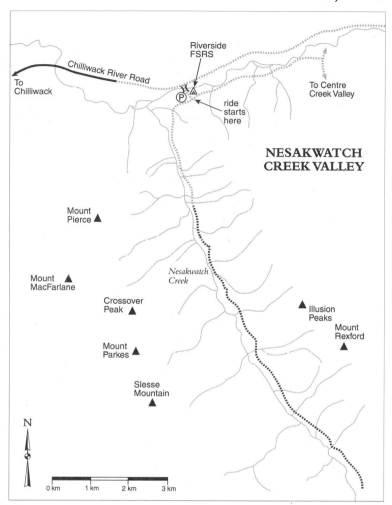

traveling on routes in this area will likely entail some bush-crashing. On the descent, views of the Cheam Range to the north open up.

The most commanding feature of the valley is Slesse Mountain. Its granite spires and buttresses point sharply skyward, prompting one to wonder how climbers can actually climb to the summit. Originally, Slesse's northern aspect was scoped out by the irrepressible U.S. climber Fred Beckey. After several attempts, his party gained the 2,375-meter summit by the classic northeast buttress in 1959. For years this mountain route was heralded as the hardest climb around. In the 1980s, this route was climbed in winter by Seattle climbers Kit Lewis and Jim Nelson over the course of eight days.

Slesse Mountain, the 2,375-meter granite guardian of the Nesakwatch Valley

The mountain also has a somewhat malevolent history. In 1956, during inclement winter weather, a DC-3 crashed into the north side of Slesse, killing all sixty-two people on board. A memorial to the passengers and crew is located near the bridge crossing the Chilliwack River at Tamihi Rapids.

APPROACH

From Vancouver, take Trans-Canada Highway 1 east to Chilliwack. Turn right at Cultus Lake–Sardis exit 119. Drive 5 kilometers south to Sardis and the metal truss bridge (zero your odometer). Turn left on the Chilliwack River Road and head east up the Chilliwack River Valley.

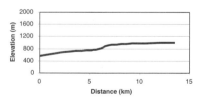

Travel 10 kilometers and cross the Chilliwack River at Tamihi Rapids. Pass by Slesse Creek at 21 kilometers and turn right at the 31-kilometer mark; cross the Chilliwack River and park near the River-side FSRS.

DISTANCE/ELEVATION LOG

0km	560m	From the parking area, turn right for Nesakwatch Creek.
3km	700m	View of Mount Pierce to the north and Mount MacFarlane to the south.
5km	750m	Old wash-out up a short hill. Valley opens.
5.2km	760m	Good view of Mount Rexford.
6.1km	820m	Views of Slesse Mountain.
6.6km	900m	Cruise uphill through recent logging. Cheam Range to the north.
8.1km	950m	Valley opens. Riding levels out.
13.5km	1,000m	Road ends at the head of the valley.

Pedal Greasing System

Most of the pedals produced today have a decent bearing system that will last for a good length of time. But if you want to increase their life, do the following: Remove the plastic end cap from the ends of the pedals. Drill a small 1- to 3-mm hole through the plastic cap. Force-thread a short (2- to 3-mm) machine screw into the new hole (make sure that the screw is slightly larger in diameter than the hole you drilled). Thread the cap back onto the pedal.

Then go to any hardware store and pick up a needle-tip grease gun attachment. Now, whenever you want to overhaul your pedals, remove the small screw and pump the grease in. Keep pumping until you see it come out the other side of the pedal, then wipe off the excess grease and re-install the screw. Simple.

30 VEDDER MOUNTAIN

Loop trips:	10km, 20km	Season:	April to November
Duration:	1 to 4 hours	Terrain:	RG50% and ST50%, or RG100%
Elevation gain:	380m	Rating:	Easy; singletrack, Moderate
High point:	580m	Map:	92-H/4

For an escape from the city for a few hours and a quick, quality mountain bike fix, come to Vedder Mountain. The area has multiple loops suitable for all abilities. Both hard-core riders who need to hammer singletrack and families who prefer more relaxing terrain will find

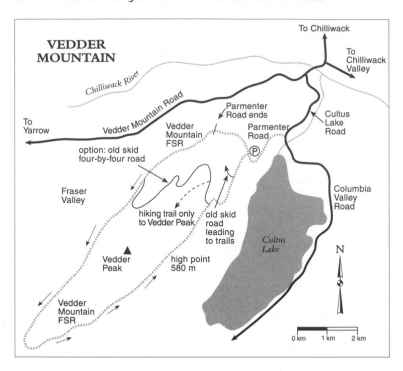

that Vedder Mountain can meet their expectations.

Vedder Mountain is located very near the entrance of the Chilliwack River Valley. It stands separate from the ranges that dominate the area. One can imagine the 930-meter mountain as an island in the rivers of prehistoric ice that flowed down the Fraser and Chilliwack Valleys. Isolated, in part because of the glacial molding, Vedder Mountain has a less robust shape than the surrounding peaks. It's actually quite hill-like, which makes it an accessible cycling destination.

Easy terrain also let the forests of Vedder Mountain fall victim to logging in the late 1930s. Skid roads fan out in all directions, serving as links to numerous established singletrack trails that are especially prominent on the mountain's north end. The major road link is Vedder Mountain FSR, which circumnavigates the mountain with Parmenter Road and acts as a catchment artery for all the harder trails that come down the mountain. It also provides an easy 20-kilometer outing for riders who are not technically inclined.

Experienced bikers can enjoy singletrack via a spur 1.3 kilometers south up Vedder Mountain FSR from the Parmenter Road intersection. The uphill grind is steep for about a kilometer, to where a small skid road intersects on the right. Push for 100 meters, then launch into

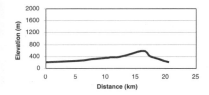

a 3-kilometer downhill run that exits on Parmenter Road near the intersection. Many variations are possible in this area. Several repeated loops can easily supply a cardio hit for the day.

For a mellower cycling experience, head west on Parmenter Road from the intersection. In 5 kilometers, Vedder Mountain FSR begins. Follow it around the mountain for another 15 kilometers, back to the Vedder-Parmenter intersection starting point.

APPROACH

From Vancouver, take Trans-Canada Highway 1 east to Chilliwack. Turn right at Cultus Lake–Sardis exit 119. Drive 5 kilometers south to Sardis and cross the Chilliwack River on a metal truss bridge. In 300 meters, turn left at the lights and zero your odometer; this marks the beginning of Cultus Lake Road.

Travel 2.2 kilometers and turn right onto Parmenter Road. At 2.8 kilometers, keep right on Parmenter Road. At 3.4 kilometers, reach the Vedder Mountain FSR/Parmenter Road intersection and park.

Easy late-season riding above the Columbia Valley

DISTANCE/ELEVATION LOG

0km	200m	Vedder Mountain FSR/Parmenter Road intersection. Head right (west) on Parmenter Road, cycling a gentle hill.
5km	250m	Follow the main road. Parmenter Road ends and Vedder Mountain FSR begins. Option: Intersection of old four-by-four road from the east. Rejoins Vedder Mountain FSR in 5.5km, at 17.5km/400m.
10km	350m	Southern limit of circumnavigation.
12.5km	400m	Great lookout over Columbia Valley and Cultus Lake.
16.2km	580m	High point.
17.5km	400m	Follow the main road. Option: Intersection of old four-by-four road from the west. Rejoins Vedder Mountain FSR in 5.5km.
20.5km	200m	Vedder Mountain FSR/Parmenter Road intersection. End of ride at the vehicle.

OPTION: VEDDER MOUNTAIN SINGLETRACK

Note: Do not ride Vedder Mountain singletrack when wet. Overuse in wet conditions kills trails.

0km	200m	Vedder Mountain FSR/Parmenter Road intersection. Turn left (south) up a steep hill.
1.3km	300m	Old skid road with numerous singletrack options to the right. Trails exit near the Vedder Mountain FSR/Parmenter Road intersection.
3km	400m	Four-by-four road; keep right (west) at the Vedder Trail junction. For connecting singletrack options— explore. A traverse of Vedder Mountain FSR is rejoined in 5.5km if this old four-by-four road is followed straight through.

Waterbottle Keepers

Ever return from a ride to find your waterbottle missing? Use a heavy duty rubberband to remedy the problem. Try recycling an old inner tube to create a rubber band by cutting the tube crossways. Half-hitch the rubberband through the bottle holder and pull tight; then clip the lid of the bottle through the loop, and—voila! You've got your keeper.

SIMILKAMEEN

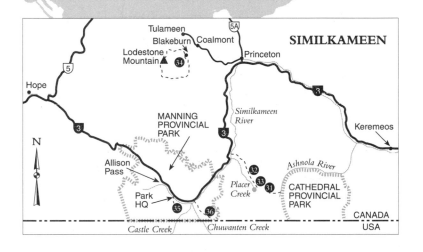

*A*dventurous mountain riders will appreciate the Similkameen region for its variety of routes. High open alpine valleys, grasslands, and mountain summits deliver trails high on scenics. The landscape is very similar to the foothills of the Rocky Mountains. The area combines both singletrack and primitive roads and will provide a premium experience for those who venture here.

The climate in the Similkameen is dry, having been sheltered by the rainshadow effect of the Coast Mountains. During the summer, temperatures can be quite warm, so drink water to avoid dehydration. The alpine areas of Manning Park and the Placer Complex can offer a welcome respite from the hot weather at lower elevations, but remember that at higher elevations, afternoon summer thunderstorms can be common.

This is cattle country, so watch for roving bovine herds and associated detritus. Respect rangeland by closing cattle gates. Drinking water in the area is suspect, so bring your own or bring a filter.

The grasslands of the high alpine are very sensitive, so be both wise and ecologically sound by keeping to established tracks. Be aware of the potential of contaminating other grassland areas by transferring noxious weeds to other regions. These plants may grow profusely in other locales and may eventually interfere with cattle nutrient intake. Help eliminate the problem by cleaning your bike of debris before leaving the area. Also be aware of ticks in the spring and rattlesnakes in the summer. Mountain biking is not permitted in nearby Cathedral Provincial Park.

The Placer Complex is a largely undiscovered mountain bike area in the mountains between Manning and Cathedral Provincial Parks. If you are even a little adventurous, you'll welcome the qualities of this interior drybelt area. Horse trails, primitive jeep roads, and logging roads combine to provide some of the best outback single- and doubletrack riding available.

Accessible mountaintops, open meadows, and valleys present a tremendous amount of fun riding. A variety of challenges makes the cycling interesting. Valley cruising, technical sections, mudholes, and even the local bovine population add atmosphere to this bonus area.

Rides can be linked for fantastic, long cross-country loops, or can be done singly as out-and-back day trips. High points are sometimes in excess of 2,200 meters, so be prepared for mountain weather and views. Interconnected game paths may test your routefinding abilities and perhaps yield a new route. Exploration possibilities abound; maps and a compass are required.

Interior scenics with alpine vistas show the expanse of land and make you feel you're in the wild. So when your heart slows after a long pump, find a peaceful lake, sit back, close your eyes, and "hear the text that nature has to render."

Note: This interior area receives a lot of equestrian traffic. On encountering horses, dismount and let them pass. Equine beasts are sensitive to the steel steed, and have been known to become extremely skittish. Horses and hikers always have the right of way.

31 TRAPPER LAKE

Round trip: 22km	Season: June to October
Duration: 3 to 4 hours	Terrain: ST100%
Elevation gain: 730m	Rating: Difficult
High point: 1,960m	Maps: 92-H/1, 92-H/2

This out-and-back route is all singletrack and promises a variety of challenges and thrills to experienced mountain riders. Roots, mudholes, bogs, rock ledges, and steep switchbacks all combine to produce a ride that delivers. Here is your chance to see how you fare on a fun but difficult test piece. Go for a swim on arrival at the lake, then rest or cast for trout. On the return, pay maximum attention to

Typical rangeland terrain of the Similkameen ©Tomas Vrba

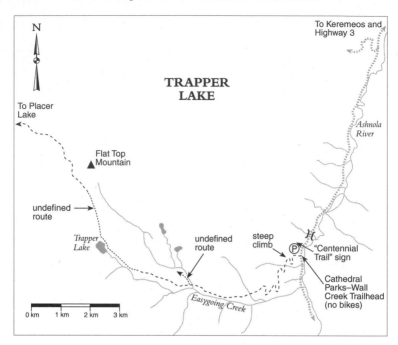

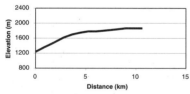

the technical ground and be sure to avoid the steaming bovine pies that can litter the trail. Whoops of excitement will emanate from your soul, but keep your mouth closed. Goggles are a good idea. At the bottom, a dip in the Ashnola River makes the day complete.

APPROACH

From Keremeos on Highway 3, drive 3 kilometers west and turn south onto Ashnola River Road (CATHEDRAL LAKES LODGE sign; zero your odometer here). Cross the Similkameen River. Head south and follow Ashnola River Road for 10.5 kilometers and cross a bridge to the west side of the Ashnola River. Ashnola FSR begins here. Continue for 50.5 kilometers and park by the CENTENNIAL TRAIL sign.

DISTANCE/ELEVATION LOG

0km 1,230m Join the trail that heads up the west side of the mountain. Expect a steep and sandy climb with some hike-and-bike here. In less than an hour the trail levels.

6.7km 1,840m Stay left; follow the red markers. Alternate through meadows and pine forest.

9km 1,860m Carefully follow the last 1.6km to Trapper Lake. Trail is vague.

10.6km 1,959m Trapper Lake. Undefined trail continues to Flat Top Mountain and Border Peak. You'll need a map and compass if you choose to continue.

32 PLACER MOUNTAIN

Round trip: 56km
Duration: 3 to 4 hours
Elevation gain: 1,265m
High point: 2,210m

Season: July to October
Terrain: RG70%, GG10%, DT20%
Rating: Moderate
Maps: 92-H/1, 92-H/2

Great open interior pine forest and a rolling road give an enjoyable afternoon of cruising. In the spring, a wealth of Indian paintbrush and Arctic lupine add a colorful palette to the scrubby undergrowth. The mountains are rounded in this area and contrast with the jagged peaks of the Cascades. Contouring up the side of Placer Mountain, the ride is short, level sections interspersed with short, steep climbs. The overall

Cruising through the high, open meadows of the interior grasslands
©Tomas Vrba

climb is very easy, with the last 5 kilometers to the 2,300-meter summit requiring the most endurance. It's worth it, though, and you can salivate over the singletrack possibilities in the area while you view all the peaks from the Coquihalla to the American Cascades.

APPROACH

From Hope, follow Highway 3 east through Manning Park. From

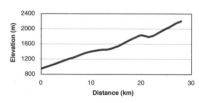

the East Gate (there's a bear carving on the sign), drive 10 kilometers (21 kilometers east of Manning Park Headquarters) and turn right on a hairpin bend in the highway at Copper Creek. Placer Mountain FSR starts here; park and ride.

From Princeton, drive 47 kilometers west on Highway 3 to access Copper Creek and Placer Mountain FSR.

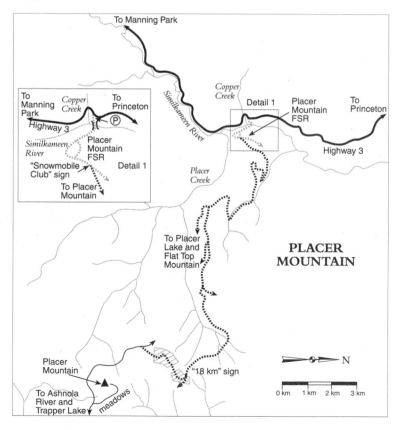

DISTANCE/ELEVATION LOG

0km	945m	Cross the Similkameen River. Start climbing gently through the open pine forest. Stay right at 0.7km and 1.7km (by the snowmobile club sign).
9.8km	1,400m	Stay left and travel along the ridge. Right goes to Placer Lake and Flat Top Mountain.
11.3km	1,390m	Stay left.
13.9km	1,480m	Stay right on the main road.
19.4km	1,921m	Turn right into the small cutblock just after the 18km sign. The road becomes rough and traverses the base of another cutblock before descending into the forest.
21.7km	1,940m	Turn left, up the west side of Placer Mountain.
26km	2,090m	Turn left onto the steep doubletrack. Follow it through the meadows and head for the faint ridge and the peak of Placer Mountain.
28km	2,210m	Summit. Excellent panorama.

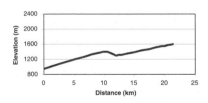

33 PLACER LAKE

Round trip: 43km
Duration: 3-plus hours
Elevation gain: 655m
High point: 1,600m

Season: July to October
Terrain: RG90%, DT5%, ST5%
Rating: Moderate
Maps: 92-H/1, 92-H/2

If you have an afternoon to spare, this outing will be perfect for you. Placer Lake is serenely nestled among forested mountainsides. This out-and-back ride is straightforward with a few waterbars and mudholes. The final 1.5 kilometers, where the road gains elevation, requires some technical riding. All the way, the pine forest is open and beautiful.

APPROACH

From Hope, follow Highway 3 east through Manning Park. From the East Gate (there's a bear carving on the sign), drive 10 kilometers (21 kilometers east of Manning Park Headquarters) and turn right on a hairpin bend in the highway at Copper Creek. Placer Mountain FSR starts here; park and ride.

From Princeton, drive 47 kilometers west on Highway 3 to access Copper Creek and Placer Mountain FSR.

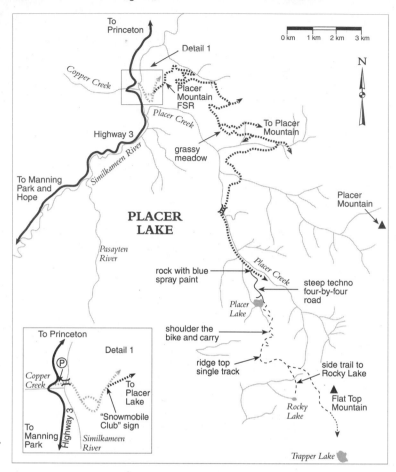

DISTANCE/ELEVATION LOG

0km	945m	Cross the Similkameen River. Start climbing gently through the open pine forest. Stay right at 0.7km and 1.7km (by the SNOWMOBILE CLUB sign).
7.9km	1,370m	Stay right.
9.8km	1,400m	Stay right and descend through the grassy meadows into the valley. Left goes to Placer Mountain.
11.8km	1,310m	Stay left and ride through the pine forest.
12.1km	1,300m	Stay right. Road levels after a short descent. Exit the forest and ride the logged valley bottom. Stay right at 15.3km and 15.6km. Cross a small creek and follow the deteriorating road up the valley. Stick to the main road.

20.3km 1,570m Turn right at the rock marked with blue spray paint. Re-enter the forest and climb a very steep, rough four-by-four road. Rocky ledges will challenge your uphill climbing technique.

21.5km 1,600m Reach Placer Lake.

A "hone-meister" takes on technical terrain on the way to Placer Lake
©Tomas Vrba

OPTION: FLAT TOP MOUNTAIN VIA PLACER LAKE

After reaching Placer Lake, advanced riders may continue on to Flat Top Mountain (2,210m), reached in 6.5 kilometers. The steep climb is a grunt, followed by a hoof with the bike on the shoulder for 45 minutes! Most will prefer to hike to the top. Regardless of the mode of transport, the destination is scenic and alpine. Views into nearby provincial parks and farther south into the Cascades will make you wish you had brought the camera.

Chain Lubrication

Your bike's chain is the key link in the drive train. Without it, you don't move. Your chain should be kept clean. Cleaning your chain will decrease wear, decrease the chance of breakage and early replacement, and eliminate any irritating chain noise. Clean it periodically with a biodegradable solvent. Clean and lubricate the chain more if you've been riding in wet, muddy conditions. There are several different types of oil available. If your budget can handle it, graphite oils are state of the art, or you can just use 30-weight oil, which is much cheaper.

34 LODESTONE MOUNTAIN/BADGER CREEK LOOP

Loop trip: 41km	Season: July to October
Duration: 4 hours	Terrain: RG70%, DT30%
Elevation gain: 1,000m	Rating: Difficult
High point: 1,850m	Map: 92-H/7

The backwaters of Princeton have yielded this lengthy cross–country gem. The 40-kilometer loop will make you want to come back again. Smooth, rolling interior hills combine with technical four–by–four ground to make a mountain bike route that is both interesting and satisfying.

Open countryside with groves of pine forest mixed with poplar and aspen define the landscape. The rounded, meadowed mountains here are an anomaly, and suggest terrain similar to eastern Canada. Through the trees, however, you may glimpse the far-off peaks of the Coquihalla to reaffirm that you really are in British Columbia.

The recreation site midway at Lodestone Lake makes a great lunch spot. There are fish here, so you may want to plan ahead and bring a rod. Judging by the number of mosquitoes that infest the area, fly fishing might give the best results. Depending on the time of year, a liberal coating of repellent may be needed. Otherwise your group will become meals-on-wheels.

Vehicle traffic is rarely a problem. Watch for mudholes that mechanical beasts have created. Some are seemingly bottomless but easily avoided. Rider splashdowns can occur when murky depths are misjudged. Exploration off this route may present other options and therefore deserve a poke. Multi-day trips can be done in the area via Whipsaw Creek, traversing Kettle and Granite Mountains.

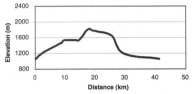

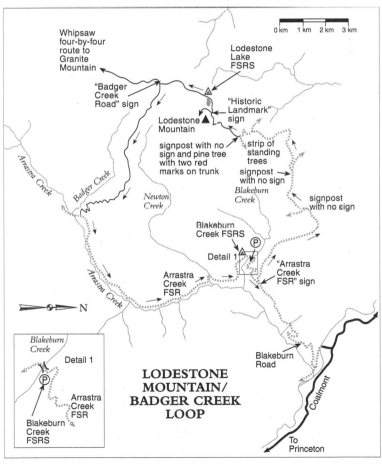

Steep terrain cruising while avoiding the mosquitoes ©Tomas Vrba

APPROACH

From Princeton, turn left off Highway 3 just before the blue truss bridge onto Bridge Street. Drive through downtown and cross the Tulameen River on a single-lane bridge. Turn left onto Tulameen Avenue and drive to the small town of Coalmont. At the first four-way stop, turn left onto Main Street, then right onto Bettes Street. Cross another single-lane bridge over the Tulameen River and turn left onto Blakeburn Road. Turn right at a stop sign (19 kilometers from Princeton) and follow Blakeburn Road for 6 kilometers up the mountain. Turn left on Arrastra Creek FSR (sign), descend to Blakeburn Creek, and park at the Blakeburn Creek Forest Service Recreation Site (FSRS).

DISTANCE/ELEVATION LOG

0km   1,050m   Ride back to the ARRASTRA CREEK FSR sign.

2.5km   1,210m   Turn left and keep climbing.

8.6km   1,450m   Stay right at the signpost with no sign.

9.5km   1,530m   Stay left at another signpost with no sign just before the 13-km marker. Ride through the young alder forest and enter a large cutblock.

13.5km   1,530m   Stay left and climb through the 100m-wide strip of standing trees.

14.5km   1,600m   Go right at the signpost with no sign by a small pine tree with two red markers on the trunk. The road heads through the forest and switchbacks to Lodestone Lake. Stick to main road.

17.3km   1,850m   Stay right at the HISTORIC LANDMARK sign.

17.9km   1,800m   Pass by the Lodestone Lake FSRS.

20.4km 1,760m Turn left onto Badger Creek Road (sign on a tree) and cruise along this twisty, mudhole-infested road through the pine forest at the edge of the mountain.
29.4km 1,200m Turn left onto Arrastra Creek FSR. Stick to main road.
41.4km 1,050m Ride ends at the parking lot.

35 WINDY JOE

Round trip: 15km	Season: July to October
Duration: 2 hours	Terrain: DT100%
Elevation gain: 522m	Rating: Moderate
High point: 1,822m	Map: 92-H/2

The moist marine climate of the coast is left behind as you drive east from Hope for 66 kilometers to Allison Summit in Manning Park. The drier weather in conjunction with the rolling topography has helped to produce pine and spruce forests interspersed with open meadows. The riding here is scenic and well-flowered, especially in the spring and early summer.

At present, B.C. Parks has opened only a handful of rides to the public. This ride and the following, Monument 83, are adventurous and fun, and give a good representation of the park.

The old, gazebo-like forest fire lookout on top of Windy Joe

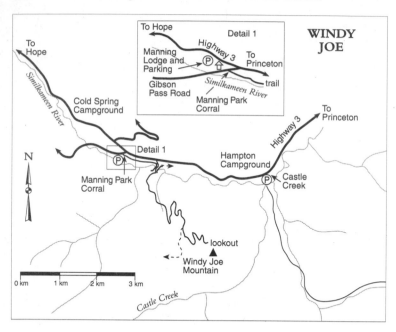

Windy Joe is an out-and-back venture that provides remarkable views of the central portion of the park. The summit of Windy Joe is at 1,822 meters and requires an elevation gain of 525 meters. The climb

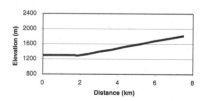

is worth the exertion. If it's windy on top, you can take shelter in the spacious old fire lookout. The funky little gazebo-like tower was built in the 1950s. The windows provide a full 360-degree panorama of the northern Cascade Range.

This fire access road climbs on a hard-packed surface through an interior pine forest before opening to subalpine terrain. The climb is invigorating and guaranteed to provide a fast descent. Check your brakes, wear goggles for the bugs, and pay heed to the hikers.

Note: As in most provincial parks, trails tend to be heavily used, especially on weekends and holidays. Expect hikers and equestrian traffic on the trail at any time. Be courteous.

APPROACH

Drive Highway 3 east from Hope to the summit of Allison Pass in 66 kilometers. Manning Provincial Park headquarters are 1 kilometer east, past the Manning Park Lodge complex on the north side of the highway. Park in the lodge lot and cycle 200 meters south, crossing the Gibson Pass Road to the Manning Park Corral.

DISTANCE/ELEVATION LOG

0km 1,300m Start at the east side of the Manning Park Corral. Follow the flow of the Similkameen River east. Note the BEAVER POND sign.

2km 1,300m Turn right and cross the Similkameen River and follow the fire road.

7.5km 1,822m Summit of Windy Joe.

36 MONUMENT 83

Round trip: 32km   Season: July to October
Duration: 4.5 hours   Terrain: DT100%
Elevation gain: 875m   Rating: Moderate
High point: 2,000m   Map: 92-H/2

Following Monument 83 to its end will place you at the extreme southeast corner of Manning Park. The American border on the 49th Parallel will be your terminus at 2,000 meters. This out-and-back 32-kilometer excursion will entertain riders of all abilities. Wilderness values are high and the trip is well worth the foray.

Riding the high country in southern Manning Provincial Park ©Tomas Vrba

As the fire road progresses, it degenerates into a rough track. The first 8 kilometers following Chuwanten Creek are the widest and most

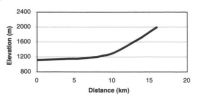

gradual. After crossing the creek, the route turns and climbs east, following Monument Creek directly to the southern high point. Remember you're in the wilderness, and ride safely. Hiking out in a damaged state wouldn't be much fun.

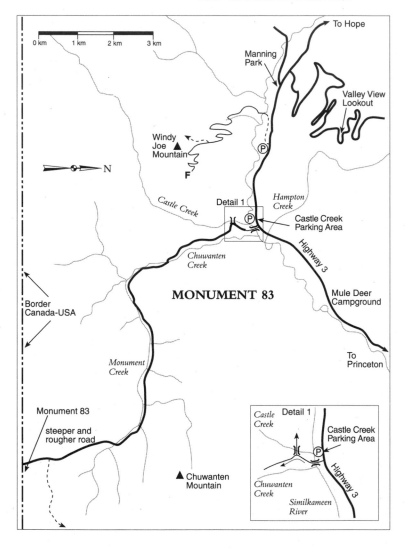

APPROACH

Drive Highway 3 east from Hope to the summit of Allison Pass in 66 kilometers. The provincial park headquarters are 1 kilometer east, past the Manning Park Lodge complex on the north side of the highway. From the Manning Park Lodge complex, drive east along Highway 3 for 3.4 kilometers to the Monument 83 Trailhead and turn right into the Castle Creek Parking Area.

DISTANCE/ELEVATION LOG

0km	1,125m	Park and cross the Similkameen River.
0.5km	1,150m	Stay left; do not cross the bridge at Castle Creek.
8km	1,200m	Head left (east) to Monument Creek, leaving Chuwanten Creek behind.
12km	1,500m	The final 4km are on a steeper and rougher fire road.
16km	2,000m	Park boundary and the American border.

Cleaning Your Bike

In a perfect world, the best way to clean your bike would be to wait for all the muck and mud to dry, then brush and rag it off—but this is not always practical. It's also time-consuming. If you do not have time to let the bike dry, you'll have to use water to remove the dirt.

Never hose off your bike with the water turned on full blast. This will move the grit into deep regions of the drive train. The last thing you want is dirt granules in the hubs and bottom bracket. Keep the water at low pressure and drool the dirt off.

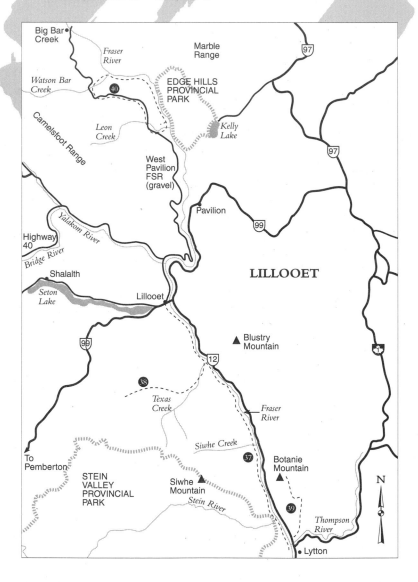

LILLOOET

Big Bar Creek

Fraser River

Marble Range

97

EDGE HILLS PROVINCIAL PARK

Watson Bar Creek

40

Kelly Lake

Leon Creek

Camelsfoot Range

97

West Pavilion FSR (gravel)

Yalakom River

Pavilion

99

Highway 40

Bridge River

LILLOOET

Shalalth

Seton Lake

Lillooet

▲ Blustry Mountain

99

12

38

Texas Creek

Fraser River

To Pemberton

Siwhe Creek

37

Botanie Mountain ▲

STEIN VALLEY PROVINCIAL PARK

Siwhe Mountain ▲

Stein River

39

Thompson River

N

• Lytton

*T*he Fraser River dominates the landscape in this region. This natural pathway was used by aboriginals, explorers, and prospectors to reach deep into the hinterland of pre-twentieth-century British Columbia. You can explore the Fraser from Lytton to Lillooet and beyond to Watson Bar Creek. Exploration by bicycle was not entertained as a method of wilderness travel 100 years ago, but today the biking possibilities are endless. Prepare for new vistas of a pioneer landscape.

The Fraser/Lillooet region gives an excellent cross-section of riding from the lowlands to the super-alpine. Comparable to the southern interior in climate, this region has the additional characteristic of granting the mountain bike rider a first-hand feel for high, rugged, remote alpine topography. You may have to work for the privilege of celebrating the view, but the toil will be well worth the effort.

The high rangeland north of Lytton can supply the more adventurous rider with ample opportunity for exploration and discovery. Countless kilometers of singletrack criss-cross the subalpine forest. Access roads provide a circuitous return to Lytton, traversing the northern flanks of Botanie Mountain. Experience with backcountry travel and the ability to use both map and compass are essential.

The coastal rainshadow gives the region an arid environment. Dehydration and hyperthermia are both possible in summer, so take lots of water and avoid overexertion during very hot weather. Traction in some instances can be unstable because of sandy deposits of glacial and riverine alluvials. You always wanted those cut quads, right?

Stellar alpine views exist in the Molybdenite/Texas Creek and Botanie Mountain areas. It's possible to reach elevations of 2,000 meters or more, which give the biker breezy refuge from the valley heat. Spring wildflowers are especially profuse in the Botanie/Laluwissen area.

Note: The Molybdenite/Texas basin has been known to host a healthy grizzly bear population. Make sure they know you are there. Also be aware of ticks in the spring and rattlesnakes in the summer.

37 LYTTON TO LILLOOET

Point to point:	67km	Season:	March to November
Duration:	1 to 2 days	Terrain:	GG65%, RG35%
Elevation gain:	1,000-plus m	Rating:	Moderate
High point:	400m	Maps:	92-I/5, 92-I/12

This well-graded, often narrow backcountry road provides a unique view of the first upriver leg of the Fraser River, just before the clear, blue waters of the Thompson River enter at Lytton. The route is an enjoyable, moderate point-to-point tour that can be done on either a mountain bike or a beefy hybrid.

The track has been in use since the 1860s, when the first farms in the area were established and prospectors ventured to the gold rush. Old cemeteries, homesteads, and the odd religious mission give the trip an historic flavor. Green farms also punctuate the otherwise dry benchlands. As well, there are glimpses of the region's twentieth-century cash crop, ginseng, covered by hectares of black shade cloth.

The maintained, undulating road wends its way through cattle rangeland, across verdant spring meadows, and close to precipices that drop straight to the Fraser River. Be wary of vehicles coming around narrow, one-lane corners. There are no guard rails and the drops are long and steep. When mixed with water, the old alluvial deposition turns into a fine, slippery, sticky mud. Plan your trip for dry weather. Fences often exist in lieu of cattle guards; be sure to close them after passing through.

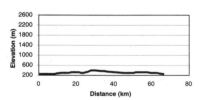

Lytton and Lillooet are often high-temperature spots in the summer. Heated hills can induce a dry heave or hork, especially when the breeze is mixed with fine dust. Keep your fluid intake at a premium. To the north, above the Stein River, are six major creeks of pristine water.

The trip can be done as a large loop connecting with Highway 12 on the east side of the Fraser, or it can be retraced. Or arrangements can be made to shuttle vehicles. If you're considering a loop, remember that you'll have to cross the Fraser via reaction ferry from Lytton. This small, bargelike ferry is unique, using the current of the river for propulsion. Check ahead for running times. Whichever way you do it, the tour is scenic and little-traveled.

Looking north toward Lillooet on the west side of the Fraser River

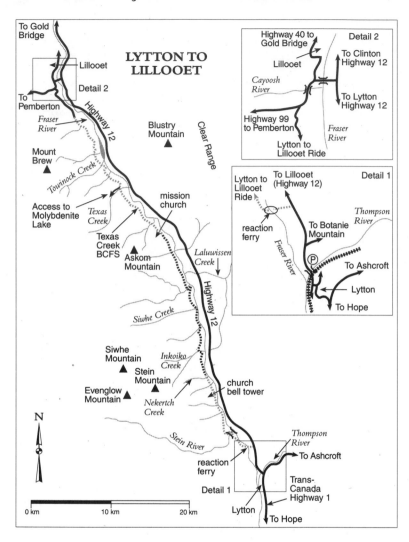

APPROACH

Turn off Trans-Canada Highway 1 at Lytton and continue north on Highway 12. Cross the one-lane Thompson River Bridge and park in the vicinity of the cabled reaction ferry. This ferry will take you across the Fraser River. Hours of operation for the ferry are 6:30 A.M. to 10:00 P.M., but it may be closed in times of high water; call (250) 387-9355. A shuttle vehicle may be dropped in Lillooet for the point-to-point tour. Highway 12 is the quickest route to Lillooet.

DISTANCE/ELEVATION LOG

0km	250m	Thompson River Bridge. Lytton, ancient site of the Indian village Camchin, which means "great fork."
1.8km	250m	Turn left. Take the reaction ferry west across the Fraser River.
3.4km	250m	Van Winkle flat; Earlscourt Farms, in operation since 1897.
7.7km	250m	Bridge over the Stein River; access here via the Stein River Valley to the old Cottonwood Creek Mine near Blowdown Pass used as a packhorse route in the 1930s.
9.8km	275m	Church bell tower and cemetery; no trespassing.
14km	300m	Nekertch Creek.
20.8km	320m	Inkoiko Creek
26.2km	350m	Tight switchback road; soon becomes sandy.
27.7km	400m	Siwhe Creek crossing.
33km	370m	Alluvial fan of Laluwissen Creek seen across the Fraser River.
41.1km	315m	Old Anglican Mission Church.
49.1km	290m	Texas Creek British Columbia Forest Service (BCFS) campsite 2km up the road. Access to Molybdenite Lake.
53.8km	330m	Towinock Creek. View of a large burn across the Fraser River on Blustry Mountain.
61.6km	310m	Pavement begins.
66.6km	250m	Junction: Lillooet to the right, Highway 99 (Duffey Lake Road) to the left.

38 MOLYBDENITE LAKE

Round trip:	36km or 40km	Season: July to October
Duration:	6 hours; Ridge option, 7 hours	Terrain: RG50%, DT30%, ST20%
Elevation gain:	1,750m; Ridge option, 2,210m	Rating: Difficult
High point:	2,040m; Ridge option, 2,523m	Maps: 92-I/5, 92-I/12

Molybdenite Creek Valley gives two stellar out-and-back ride options. Contrast in terrain and climate reigns supreme on both adventures. Leaving the fluvial meander of the upper Fraser River, the route passes through a cool canyon and open forest to ascend directly to the alpine level. At Molybdenite Lake (2,100 meters), the air is crisp and cool, the water cold but inviting. On the accessible adjoining ridges you'll likely find a breezy refuge to further counter the summer valley heat.

An early start is recommended because of the area's hot, dry nature. The climb is steep to both Molybdenite Lake and the 2,500-meter Molybdenite Ridge system. The grind is of the usual character-inducing variety but the views and tempting waters more than make up for the strain. Grassy, open rangeland with pockets of purple lupine and the chatter of small animals add to the experience.

At 7 kilometers, explore up the Texas Creek drainage with its great hiking access into the northern Stein. The road continues for another 12 kilometers before ending in an old cutblock. You can do a loop ride here by carrying up the trail and crossing down into the narrow Siwhe Creek Valley. I can't recommend that horror, but the 20-minute hike onto the divide is definitely worth the effort.

At 14 kilometers, turn right and climb up the steep valley side for 2 kilometers, leaving the forest behind. Ride through vast alpine meadows. The road, now a narrow doubletrack, goes to the headwall of the valley before switchbacking up to the ridge crest. As you gain elevation the route degrades to a wide, lupine-lined singletrack. At 2,500 meters the trail ends. Hike the last few meters to the top; it's worth it.

Great views from 2,500-meter-high Molybdenite Ridge ©Tomas Vrba

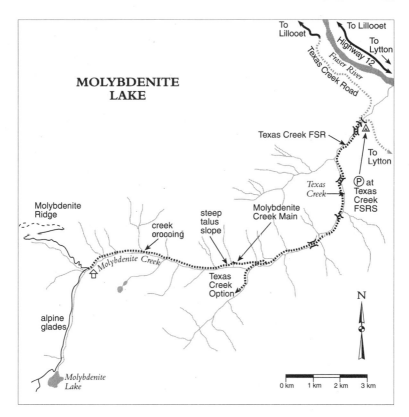

A panoramic view awaits, with some of the best scenery in southwest British Columbia.

Get pumped, for the descent is exciting and knuckle-numbing. Surrounding rock walls echo any fervent yelps. The backdrop is spectacular. You are in the mountains and you are riding! Some rocky singletrack helps tune your balance and tweak your coordination. This is rangeland, where cattle doughnuts dot the road, so keep your mouth closed and waterbottles covered. Sharp turns and fast-winding road will have you down in no time.

APPROACH

From Lillooet, drive south on Highway 99 toward Pemberton. Shortly after passing the Shell gas station, turn south (zero your odometer) on Texas Creek Road. This road traverses the benchlands on the west side of the Fraser River. Drive for 18 kilometers to the small Forest Service Recreation Site (FSRS) on the south side of Texas Creek. Park here.

DISTANCE/ELEVATION LOG

0km	290m	Cross north over Texas Creek and turn left on Texas Creek FSR. Climb up through the cool canyon, crossing the creek four times in the next 5km.
7km	920m	Turn right onto Molybdenite Creek Main. Climb up the rough road through the alder forest. Near Molybdenite Creek the road narrows and switchbacks twice before traversing a steep talus slope.
10km	1,320m	Stay left and follow the main road along Molybdenite Creek.
11.5km	1,590m	Splash through a small creek. Road levels for several km.
13.6km	1,720m	Logging road reverts back to mining road. Pass a cabin on the left.
14.1km	1,740m	Stay left for Molybdenite Lake. Ride through open alpine glades along the steep valley.
18km	2,040m	Molybdenite Lake. The mining road continues up the valley to a pass with views.

OPTION: MOLYBDENITE RIDGE

14.1km	1,750m	Turn right. Start climbing switchbacks.
16km	2,080m	Narrow doubletrack in vast meadow.
18.5km	2,340m	Narrow saddle. Great views. Trail traverses gently westward and continues to short switchbacks.
20km	2,523m	Ridge summit. Panoramic view. Excellent and worth it.

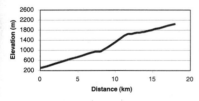

Molybdenite Lake

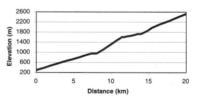

Molybdenite Ridge Option

Seven-inch Pruning Saws

Every mountain biker should have one of these handy little folding units. They easily fit into almost any fanny pack and can cut up to 14-inch-diameter blowdowns (somebody's got to clear them).

39 BOTANIE MOUNTAIN

Round trip: 25km
Duration: 4 hours
Elevation gain: 1,422m
High point: 2,042m

Season: July to October
Terrain: DT100%
Rating: Difficult
Maps: 92-I/4, 92-I/5, 92-I/6

For both physical and scenic rewards, this mountain bike ride does not
disappoint. Because this adventure works the cardio to new levels, you
should be relatively fit or you'll be struggling for air, especially near
the 2,042-meter south summit ending. The true summit is 3 kilometers to the north and only 6 meters higher.

The ride need not be done in a couple of hours, but can easily
take most of the day. In spring, the Botanie Mountain area has intense
flower bloom. May and June are the best months for maximum color.
Wildflowers are profuse and can cover the meadows completely, so
bring your camera. Indian paintbrush, tiger lily, lupine, balsam root,
and columbine are only some of the varieties to be found.

Grinding the granny toward the old fire lookout on Botanie Mountain.
©Tomas Vrba

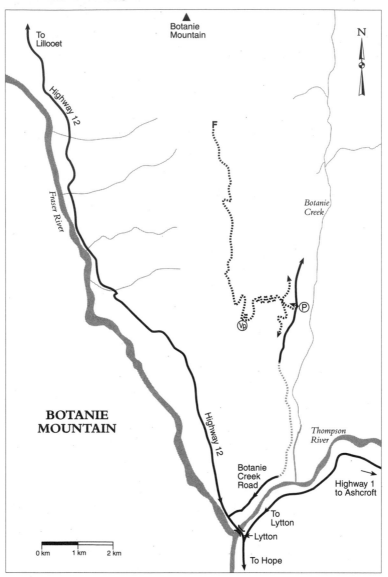

The views are exceptional. At the summit are interesting perspectives: to the north, the Clear Range; to the west, the Stein River; to the east, the Scarped Range; and to the south, a panorama of the Fraser Canyon.

Botanie Mountain was originally named by local aboriginals as Bootahnie, for clouds that often lingered above it. If there is a dark cloud hanging over Botanie Mountain, it is its big elevation gain, which is slightly more than 1,400 meters. The riding itself is straight-forward. Some of the switchbacks are littered with loose gravel, which tends to be slippery. Bouldery rocks near the summit demand more technical riding. Water is a concern, especially when the weather is hot. Take lots of water to avoid dehydration.

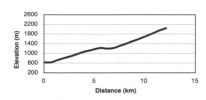

The challenging nature of this recommended mountain bike adventure can make you feel larger than life when you stand on the summit.

APPROACH

From Lytton, follow Highway 12 north. Cross the single-lane bridge over the Thompson River. In 300 meters, turn right onto Botanie Creek Road. It quickly changes to gravel and climbs. Pavement resumes when the road levels. After 7 kilometers, turn left onto a small dirt side road (easily missed). Park and start riding.

DISTANCE/ELEVATION LOG

0km   620m   Follow the faint track through the sparse pine forest on a gentle grade.

0.2km   620m   Stay right and enter a dense forest.

0.6km   630m   Turn left and cross an old irrigation ditch. Granny-out up steep switchbacks. Loose rocks make this a challenging climb.

3.5km   1,010m Stop and enjoy the view from the ridge crest.

5.5km   1,220m Enter another dense pine forest. The road levels for 1.5km before the final ascent up the ridge. Steep and rough.

12.2km 2,042m Yes . . . the end. Old fire lookout. View the peaks above the Stein River Valley to the west, the Clear Range to the north.

OPTION: BOTANIE MOUNTAIN LOOP

Travel 18 kilometers north on Highway 12 from the single-lane Thompson River Bridge to the junction of Laluwissen FSR and turn right. After 9.8 kilometers and a 700-meter elevation gain, the road plateaus and reaches a junction. Turn right to loop around Botanie Mountain, past Pasulko and Botanie Lakes on the east side of the mountain, and back to Lytton, making a 42-kilometer loop. Great spring flowers.

40 WATSON BAR CREEK LOOP

Loop trip:	70km	Season:	March to November
Duration:	1 to 2 days	Terrain:	GG40%, DT30%, ST30%
Elevation gain:	1,500m	Rating:	Moderate
High point:	1,240m	Maps:	92-I/13, 92-P/4

This loop is one of the most interesting and aesthetically pleasing rides in the Lillooet area. In this adventure, you get a taste of what it was like to travel along the silt-laden Fraser in the 1800s. Be prepared to find evidence of homesteaders and prospectors who eked out a precarious existence here at the turn of the century.

The route is a rougher counterpart to the Lytton/Lillooet road; the trip is a much wilder experience. You will encounter single-track, doubletrack, and graded gravel road. Traffic is minimal along West Pavilion FSR. Once you drop to the Fraser itself, you may not see anyone until Watson Bar.

From Lillooet, travel 45 kilometers north on West Pavilion FSR, high above the Fraser around cliffy, dramatic hills, and through open rangeland. Views are always interesting, showing yawning canyon chasms and raging rapids. At 45 kilometers, the descent follows a rough track to farmland just above the river. Descending to river level is possible at Leon Creek. The road deteriorates to singletrack here and winds its way to Watson Bar Creek. The route travels along the river for a total of 30 undulating kilometers.

At Watson Bar a gravel road leads back to West Pavilion FSR in less than 10 kilometers, but with an elevation gain of 520 meters. This gravel road can then be followed south back to kilometer 45. The loop to the Fraser runs close to 70 kilometers—a worthwhile trip on its own. If you don't have time constraints, consider starting the ride from

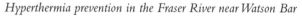

Hyperthermia prevention in the Fraser River near Watson Bar

Lillooet. You will, however, have to ride an extra 90 kilometers on the return and climb one heinous hill that will tax to the max.

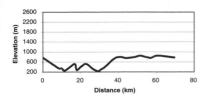

This totally recommended trip makes you appreciate the Fraser for the heritage river it is. Spend some time; an overnight trip is best. Good specimens for budding geologists, birdwatchers, and botanists abound.

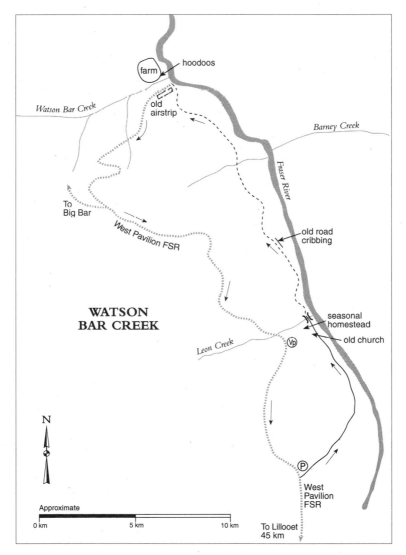

Note: This benchland is both ecologically and historically sensitive, so act accordingly. The route also crosses aboriginal land of Lillooet's Pavilion Band. Be respectful of land and property and close gates after you pass.

APPROACH

From the Lillooet townsite, drive north on Highway 40 for 9.5 kilometers to where the Bridge River flows into the Fraser. Turn right onto West Pavilion FSR. Drive (or ride for a bigger loop) up a major hill (700 meters) and across benchlands for a total of 45 kilometers from Lillooet. Park near a small side road to the east, just past a ranch and up a short hill.

DISTANCE/ELEVATION LOG

0km	770m	Ride down a small side road to the Fraser River. Start a 70km loop to Watson Bar. Descend.
4.5km	530m	Drop down switchbacks past old river silt profiles.
7.5km	370m	View of old abandoned church, homestead, and ranchland.
9km	330m	Seasonal homestead; remember to close the cattle gate.
10km	350m	Newer seasonal ranch house.
11.8km	250m	Sandy drop to Leon Creek.
16.8km	530m	Open grasslands drop to a forested glade in a bend.
18km	270m	Drop toward a rocky bluff above Fraser Push here; notice old road cribbing.
22.5km	530m	Open benchlands. Sandy travel. View the canyon to the north.
27km	300m	First view of Watson Bar.
30km	250m	Watson Bar Creek. Explore the area and marvel at the hoodoos. Camp at the unoffical campsite at the creek, or near the Fraser River.
38.7km	770m	After passing an airstrip, climb 520m to West Pavilion FSR and turn left.
70km	770m	After more than 30km of undulating variable gravel road with a high point of 1,240m, return to your vehicle.

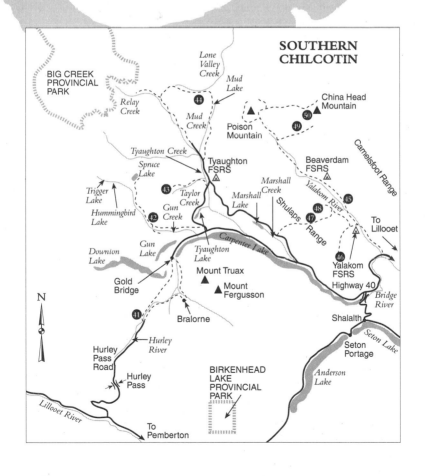

SOUTHERN CHILCOTIN

SOUTHERN CHILCOTIN

BIG CREEK PROVINCIAL PARK

Lone Valley Creek

Mud Lake

China Head Mountain

Relay Creek

Mud Creek

Poison Mountain

50

49

Tyaughton Creek

Spruce Lake

Tyaughton FSRS

Beaverdam FSRS

Camelsfoot Range

Trigger Lake

Hummingbird Lake

43

Taylor Creek

Marshall Lake

Marshall Creek

Yalakom River

45

Shulaps Range

48

47

42

Gun Creek

Downton Lake

Gun Lake

Carpenter Lake

To Lilloet

N

Tyaughton Lake

Mount Truax

46

Yalakom FSRS

Highway 40

Gold Bridge

Mount Fergusson

Bridge River

41

Bralorne

Shalalth

Hurley River

Hurley Pass Road

Hurley Pass

BIRKENHEAD LAKE PROVINCIAL PARK

Seton Portage

Seton Lake

Anderson Lake

Lillooet River

To Pemberton

*T*he southern Chilcotin, a hidden corner in the rainshadow of the Coast Range, represents all that adventure mountain biking can be. Less than five hours from Vancouver, Gold Bridge, the small settlement at the southern edge of the Chilcotin Mountains, is reached from Pemberton via 80 kilometers of steep gravel road through Hurley Pass, or 100 kilometers of narrow, winding road from Lillooet. The area receives surprisingly little precipitation, which translates into stable weather patterns and a longer riding season because of the lack of snow.

The southern Chilcotin ranges are networked by a system of excellent horse trails with gradual gradients. Originally built by prospectors looking for the mother lode and now primarily used by outfitters, hikers, and mountain bikers, the trails are well suited to day rides, overnight trips, or longer expeditions. Hundreds of kilometers of singletrack in the southern Chilcotin, including the Shulaps and Camelsfoot Ranges, combine with outstanding wilderness to make this a mountain biker's Utopia.

A trip to the southern Chilcotin is always rewarding. The flowers begin to bloom profusely from May to July. Much of the area has high parkland and wilderness values of ample wildlife, pristine environment, exceptional scenery, biological diversity, and ecological sensitivity.

To the west of Tyaughton Lake and the Shulaps Range lies the Spruce Lake Wilderness. Containing over 100,000 hectares of wild land, it's bounded in the west by Big Creek Provincial Park and Warner Pass, in the south by Slim Creek, and in the north by Relay Creek. This area is pristine, with lakes, meadows, and rivers—and it's special. Directly in the rainshadow of the Coast Range, the environment here is similar to the drier Shulaps and Camelsfoot Ranges to the east. Groves of aspen interspersed with lush grassland flavor the topography against a backdrop of the eastern peaks of the Coast Range. This is an ecological transition zone between coastal and interior habitats. Flowers here bloom with remarkable abundance, so much so that famed University of British Columbia botanist Burt Brink says, "It is the most exceptional flower show going." Wildlife is profuse. Deer, bobcat, lynx, grizzly bear, wolverine, moose, and California bighorn sheep all roam the region.

Since 1937, the Spruce Lake Wilderness has been proposed as a park. Those who have experienced the area have found it so special, they have tended to keep quiet about it, not anticipating that one day, economic development, based on supposed lack of interest reflected in the low number of visitors to the area, would pose a threat. The original economic mandate called for logging up to the headwaters of Gun Creek near Warner Pass. This watershed is now a popular hiking and horsepack route to Spruce, Trigger, Hummingbird, and Warner Lakes. Historically, this 40-kilometer route was once the trading route of the Nemiah people of the Chilko-Taseko Lakes to the Fraser River. Despite the logging that has already occurred on the periphery, recreational values here are extremely high. Hopefully, this area will soon be given protected status before logging destroys this world-class arena.

A good overview of the area is shown on the Spruce Lake Draft Forest Service Map. Contact the Forest Service in Lillooet at (250) 256-1200 for a free copy. Using Enquiry B.C. at (604) 660-2421, the call will also be free.

World-class scenery and great wilderness values, combined with perhaps the best singletrack anywhere, make these mountains special enough to receive a place in anybody's heart. If you can, get yourself to the southern Chilcotin for the experience.

41 GOLD BRIDGE/BRALORNE LOOP

Loop trip: 42km	Season: May to November
Duration: 6 to 8 hours	Terrain: BT30%, GG40%, RG15%, DT15%
Elevation gain: 330m	Rating: Easy
High point: 1,030m	Maps: 92-J/10, 92-J/15

This ride is a good introduction to the Gold Bridge/Bralorne area. The route links three sections of road for a 42-kilometer loop, or it can broken down and ridden point-to-point or as an out-and-back trip. The terrain follows undulating foothills into the valley bottom. The steepest hill climb is from Gold Bridge south to Bralorne. The 330 meters gained here is all on pavement and is over in less than 6 kilometers. The remaining 4 kilometers to Bralorne is mostly a level cruise.

While the trip can be done in either direction, it's best to travel the first 18.5 kilometers north to Gold Bridge. This section receives quite a bit of traffic and has a lot of downhill sections that would be an unpleasant and dusty gut-wrench as a return.

Gold Bridge to Bralorne is an easy cruise once the initial hill is climbed. Although the old mine at Bralorne shut down in 1970—after operating since 1932—the old townsite is still intact and functional. More than $100 million in gold was mined here.

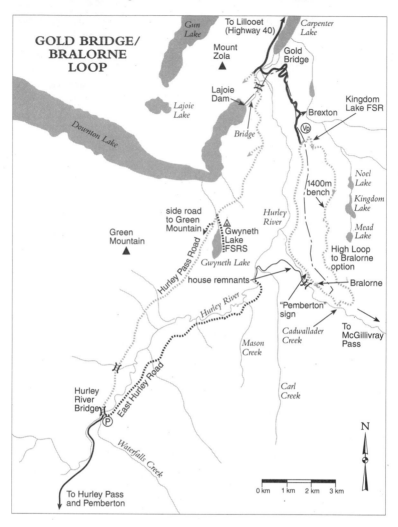

From the main intersection in Bralorne, the trail continues downhill to cross the Cadwallader Creek bridge and will eventually take you via East Hurley Road back to your vehicle. This last and most remote section of the trip begins by passing the foundations of two abandoned houses, then continues above Cadwallader Creek through a canopied forest of aspen, pine, and spruce. The four-by-four road soon narrows, returning to a primitive quality with big, water-filled holes and the odd gnarly root.

Three kilometers west of the Cadwallader Creek bridge, the road drops to the green, rushing waters of the Hurley River. Soon the track opens onto old cutblocks, then traverses an obvious avalanche slope. Another 11.6 kilometers brings you back to the vehicle. The trip is a

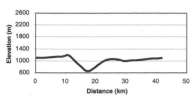

moderate half-day return pump. Two pubs en route in each of the small towns provide an opportunity to slake your thirst and chat with the friendly locals. The East Hurley Road provides a good out-and-back ride to Bralorne in about 23 kilometers, from the main Hurley intersection. You may want to venture toward McGillivray Pass from here as well. Consult the map.

APPROACH

From Pemberton, drive west 25 kilometers and turn right at Lillooet FSR (HURLEY–BRALORNE sign). Cross the valley bottom and drive over the single-lane bridge that crosses the Lillooet River. Continue west for 8 kilometers and turn uphill to Hurley Pass (1,325 meters; opens in May, closes with the first snow in October) at the GOLD BRIDGE–BRALORNE sign. Park at the major pullout beside the Hurley River Bridge, 35 kilometers from the Lillooet Bridge and 60 kilometers from Pemberton. This is the intersection of the main Hurley Pass Road that travels north to Gold Bridge in 18.5 kilometers and the rough East Hurley Road that leads east to Bralorne in 11 kilometers.

View west up the Bridge River Valley near Bralorne

DISTANCE/ELEVATION LOG

0km	1,100m	Ride north over the Hurley River Bridge.
11km	1,200m	Option: Turn left for Green Mountain (2,156m). Rough, steep four-by-four. Good views.
11.5km	1,140m	Option: Turn right for the Gwyneth Lake FSRS with camping here.
16.4km	690m	Stay right and continue downhill.
17.5km	660m	Carpenter Lake estuary. Turn right and cross Bridge River.
18.5km	700m	Gold Bridge. Get pumped for a 5km, 330m climb on pavement.
23.5km	1,030m	Stay right. High Loop option: Turn off to Kingdom Lake FSR. (Possible climb here to the 1,390m benchland toward McGillivray Pass.) The main road continues to climb for 150m.
28.5km	1,020m	Bralorne. Turn right at a small PEMBERTON sign.
28.8km	960m	Cross Cadwallader Creek, turning onto East Hurley Road.
29.4km	970m	Travel past collapsed and rundown houses from the Bralorne boon years. Road becomes primitive; carry over a small washout.
42km	1,100m	Arrive at your vehicle.

OPTION: HIGH LOOP TO BRALORNE AND MCGILLIVRAY PASS

Another shorter loop is possible via south on Kingdom Lake FSR, plateauing on a 1,400-meter-high, 7-kilometer-long bench before the road forks right to Cadwallader Creek and Bralorne. The left fork will take you a few kilometers to the Standard Creek FSRS and toward McGillivray Pass before it peters out to a flowered but boggy hiking trail.

42 GUN CREEK TO SPRUCE LAKE

Round trip:	26km via Jewel Creek Bridge/	Season: May to October
	Spruce Lake Trailhead	Terrain: ST100%
	41km via Pearson Creek	Rating: Moderate
Duration: 5 to 7 hours		Map: 92-J/15, 92-J/16, 92-O/3,
Elevation gain: 525m		and Spruce Lake Draft
High point: 1,570m		Forest Service Map

Expect scenic and ecological values on this trip to be outstanding. Riding Gun Creek to Spruce Lake as an out-and-back singletrack adventure will introduce you to only a minute fraction of the trails available in this area. The Garden of Eden atmosphere that typifies this special place requires special care, so limit the frequency and length of your visits. When encountering equestrian and hiker traffic, dismount and move off the trail. Equine beasts are super-sensitive and react skittishly to the steel steed. Common sense will go a long way to help give credence to the mountain bike community.

Starting at the Jewel Creek Bridge/Spruce Lake Trailhead, the trail parallels Gun Creek, subtly gaining elevation through a conifer forest mixed with aspen and cottonwood. There are frequent open areas along the creek for enjoying the view. At Eldorado Creek, cross a small footbridge and continue up old forested moraines before rejoining Gun Creek. The route crosses a sturdy bridge and continues up the creek. There may be a few short sections where you'll have to push the bike. Across the river, goat trails are identifiable on the cone-shaped scree slopes.

Crossing Gun Creek again, some elevation is gained until the open slopes of the alpine grasslands are reached. Early in the season this area is lush and profusely flowered. Reach the junction at 11.5 kilometers, then climb 200 meters farther in 2 kilometers to campsites east and north of Spruce Lake. You may even want to bring your fishing rod.

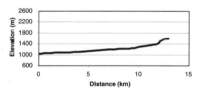

This ride is moderate, scenic, and wholly recommended. The trail is completely singletrack with few obstacles. The descent is extremely exhilarating. Your level of excitement will easily prompt joyful whoops that will warn the bears of your presence!

If you feel strongly about this area, give support to the Southern Chilcotin Mountains Wilderness Society, General Delivery, Gold Bridge, BC V0K 1P0.

APPROACH

From Gold Bridge (zero your odometer), travel downhill back to Highway 40 and the single-lane bridge that crosses the Bridge River (1km), then turn left. At 1.3 kilometers, stay right and uphill; at 2 kilometers, keep left and pass La Jolie Dam and Downton Lake before climbing up to Gun Lake. At 6.3 kilometers, stay left on the main road that continues along Gun Lake. Keep left at 14.5 kilometers on Slim Creek Main and pass a hidden airstrip. At 18.4 kilometers, stay right and descend into the Gun Creek valley. At 22.6 kilometers, turn right and park at the Jewel Creek Bridge/Spruce Lake Trailhead.

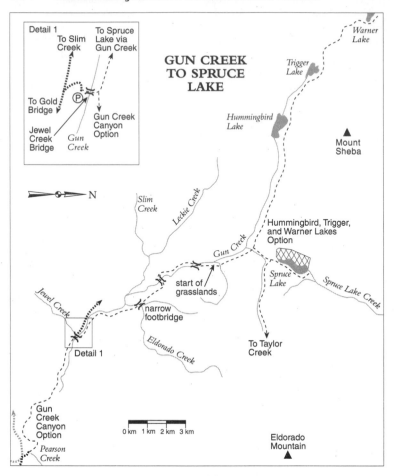

DISTANCE/ELEVATION LOG

0km   1,046m   Cross Gun Creek and follow the trail left, upstream.
                 Right goes to the Gun Creek Canyon and Pearson Creek.

0.5km   1,050m   Short carry/push across a scree slide.

4km   1,100m   Cross Eldorado Creek on a narrow footbridge.

7km   1,200m   Cross Gun Creek on a sturdy bridge.

9km   1,210m   Cross Gun Creek again and gently gain elevation
                 into alpine grasslands.

11.5km   1,380m   Turn right for Spruce Lake. Options to travel locally
                     to Hummingbird, Trigger, and Warner Lakes, and
                     ultimately, if you have several extra days, to Taseko
                     and Chilco Lakes.

13.0km   1570m   Spruce Lake.

OPTION: GUN CREEK CANYON

A loop is possible, traveling 7 kilometers of the Lower Gun Creek trail to connect with the Jewel Creek Bridge/Spruce Lake Trailhead. To access the trailhead from Gold Bridge, head east for 10 kilometers on Highway 40 to the Tyaughton Lake turnoff. Travel uphill 2 kilometers past Mowson Pond (FSRS here); at 4 kilometers, turn left onto Gun Creek Road. At 9 kilometers, cross Pearson Creek and park. Follow the singletrack along Gun Creek 7 kilometers to the Jewel Creek Bridge/Spruce Lake Trailhead. Either continue to Spruce Lake or cycle Slim Creek Main to the main paved road on Carpenter Lake (Highway 40) and complete the loop back to Pearson Creek.

43 TAYLOR PASS

Round trip:	14km	Season:	July to October
Duration:	6 hours	Terrain:	GG5%, DT95%
Elevation gain:	726m	Rating:	Moderate
High point:	1,741m	Maps:	92-O/2, 92-J/16

Years ago, mining interests prompted the construction of a rough track that wends its way into the high alpine. What remains today is a wonderfully primitive access that tops out at more than 1,700 meters. The scenics in this area are Yukonesque, with high, rounded, mineral-stained mountains that also provide some of the best hiking in southern British Columbia. Through it all runs a super-short, out-and-back ride that can easily be negotiated even by those with nominal skills.

Your trip starts in a recent cutblock set about 5 kilometers from Tyaughton Lake Road. A rough road through the slash merges with the old mining track that gradually traverses with an easy gradient to

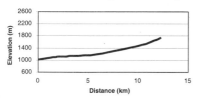

a dilapidated bridge crossing Taylor Creek. Elevation gain starts in earnest here. A further 4.5 kilometers will put you at the Taylor Creek cabin. "Mr. Taylor's fine old cabin has been re-roofed, re-floored and weatherproofed," reads the introduction in the cabin guest book. "Please enjoy this cabin and please do not take any of the tools or equipment—they are for everyone's use and enjoyment." Recently refurbished, this user-friendly cabin is a welcome place for a rest stop and a bite to eat beside gurgling Taylor Creek. The grind continues through open, flowered meadows, along

Grinding up the old mining track in the Taylor Creek Valley ©Tomas Vrba

small streams, and up switchbacks. In less than 2 kilometers you'll be standing on the summit of Taylor Pass.

The route to Taylor Pass has the added appeal of showing you some of the special qualities that make up the southern Chilcotin. This basin in particular is one of those on the list to be deleted from the wilderness study area that will hopefully see the Spruce Lake Wilderness become a park. Be an activist and let the powers-that-be know your concern!

APPROACH

From Gold Bridge (zero your odometer), head downhill to Highway 40 and cross the single-lane bridge over the Bridge River (1km). Turn right and follow Highway 40 along Carpenter Lake for 10 kilometers and turn left at the TYAX LODGE sign (Tyaughton Lake Road). Climb toward Tyaughton Lake. At 14 kilometers, stay right (Gun Creek Road is to the left). At 16.3 kilometers, stay left on the main road. At 18.3 kilometers, stay left at the TYAX LODGE sign. At 23.3 kilometers, stay right and downhill. Park at 24.5 kilometers, at the three-way junction stop sign.

DISTANCE/ELEVATION LOG

0km	1,015m	From the junction, ride up the side road to the left.
1.5km	1,100m	Stay right at the logging landing and follow an old road.
2.3km	1,125m	Stay left.
3.5km	1,140m	Turn left onto the rough track leading uphill at the second logging landing.
6km	1,200m	Cross Taylor Creek over a small collapsed bridge.
10.5km	1,520m	Taylor Cabin.
12.3km	1,741m	Taylor Pass.

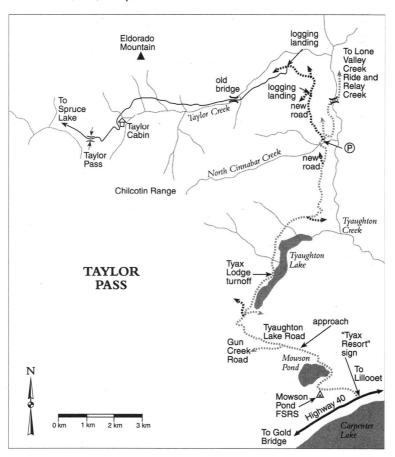

44 LONE VALLEY–RELAY CREEK LOOP

Loop trip: 56km
Duration: 6 to 8 hours
Elevation gain: 850m
High point: 1,790m

Season: June to October
Terrain: GG40%, RG20%, DT10%, ST30%
Rating: Difficult
Maps: 92-J/16, 92-0/1, 92-0/2

The character of this loop and optional out-and-back ride is almost beyond description. The views are almost off the scale. The outback feeling of the enclosed primitive road of Relay Creek, punctuated by groves of aspen, open conifer forest, and grasslands, will make you want to return. Singletrack through a hidden valley that contains its own particular ecosystem and the chance to see a variety of wildlife from moose to wolves make this area remarkable.

The recommended route is a loop from the Tyaughton Creek FSRS. Ride it clockwise or counter-clockwise; either way works well, and the elevation gain is about the same. The description here is for the counter-clockwise loop. Cycle northeast to north Mud Lake (camp spot) and reach the high point of the road in 1.8 kilometers (16.9 kilometers from the Tyaughton Creek FSRS). Then climb to a forested ridge via a steep horse track and drop into Lone Valley. Reach Prentice Lake at the head of valley in 15 kilometers of singletrack, with a bonus 3.5-kilometer run into Relay Valley. Mining road changes to ultra-smooth deactivated logging road that will have you back at the recreation site in an additional 21 kilometers.

Humungous slimy yellow "shrooms" on the Lone Valley–Relay Creek Loop

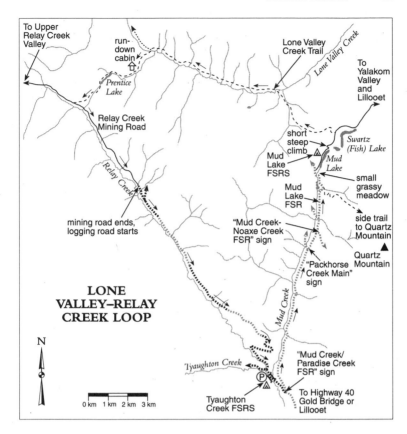

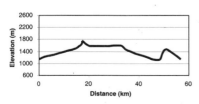

The second option, for those with limited time, can be done as an out-and-back ride from Mud Lake to Prentice Lake—a 30-kilometer, 300-vertical-meter return trip. The third option, again for those with limited time, entails access from Relay Creek. Drive as far as you want up the Relay drainage, then cycle as far as you wish (old backcountry cowboy cabin at the end of the Relay doubletrack, 28.8 kilometers from the Tyaughton Creek FSRS). This is the mellowest of the three.

Note: This relatively unknown ride has been included in this book because of impending resource development. Lone Valley Creek is slated to be logged within five years. This area is an important wildlife corridor, especially as over-wintering habitat. Logging will destroy that. Cherish the area and ride, for if the powers-that-be have their way, it will soon become history.

APPROACH

From Gold Bridge, travel east on Highway 40 from the single-lane bridge that crosses the Bridge River. At 10 kilometers, turn left to Tyax Resort and Tyaughton Lake and zero the odometer. At 8.4 kilometers, pass the Tyax Resort turnoff and continue uphill. Reach the Taylor Creek access at 13.6 kilometers and travel downhill on Mud–Taylor FSR. At 14.1 kilometers, cross Tyaughton Creek at the beginning of a short canyon. Head uphill and turn left at 15.1 kilometers onto Tyaughton–Mud FSR. Follow the main road north and turn left onto Mud Creek–Paradise Creek FSR at 22.1 kilometers. Reach the Tyaughton Creek FSRS 23.7 kilometers from Highway 40. This is the quickest approach from the west. Also makes a good cycle on its own.

From Lillooet, travel northwest on Highway 40 to Gold Bridge. Turn right at the Marshall Lake Road junction, 67 kilometers west of Lillooet (33 kilometers east of Gold Bridge). Continue uphill; at 11 kilometers, stay right at the MUD CREEK FSR sign. At 28.5 kilometers, stay left at Ainsworth–Noaxe Creek FSR, following the road down toward the Relay Valley. At 33.5 kilometers, stay right at Mud Creek FSR. At 39.5 kilometers, turn left onto Mud Creek–Paradise Creek FSR and park at the Tyaughton Creek FSRS, 42.1 kilometers.

DISTANCE/ELEVATION LOG

0km	1,150m	From Tyaughton Creek FSRS, ride south 1.6km to Mud Creek–Paradise Creek FSR.
1.6km	1,210m	Turn left onto Mud Creek–Paradise Creek FSR.
8.1km	1,300m	Stay right at the PACKHORSE CREEK MAIN sign.
9km	1,350m	Stay left at the MUD CREEK–NOAXE CREEK FSR sign.
10.3km	1,400m	Stay right. MUD CREEK FSR sign.
14.4km	1,490m	Turn right on rough four-by-four road.
15.1km	1,510m	Pass Mud Lake FSRS. The four-by-four road follows the shore of the lake and climbs steeply.
16.9km	1,640m	Road crests; look for a trail to the left. Climb it to a forested ridge, gaining 150m elevation to the high point (1,790m), and descend the north side into Lone Valley.
30.5km	1,600m	Pass a run-down cabin.
32km	1,600m	Pass Prentice Lake and descend to Relay Creek.
35.5km	1,430m	Turn left onto Relay Creek Mining Road and follow it back to the Tyaughton Creek FSRS. Option: A right turn heads to an old cowboy cabin on the upper Relay Creek Mining Road in 7km.
42km	1,250m	Mining road ends. Logging road begins.

50.7km 1,500m After traveling ultra-smooth deactivated logging
road, prepare for a 6km, 500m descent.

56.7km 1,150m Arrive at the Tyaughton Creek FSRS.

45 YALAKOM VALLEY

Round trip:	98km (variable)	Season:	May to October
Duration:	8 hours	Terrain:	GG100%
Elevation gain:	1,300m	Rating:	Moderate
High point:	1,700m	Maps:	92–J/16, 92-0/1, 92–0/2

The Yalakom Valley Road is a perfect introduction to the vast offerings
of the southern Chilcotin. If you have the time, this route will provide
the opportunity to explore a remote valley steeped in history. This 49-
kilometer valley is a good out-and-back ride, or if you are short on
time, consider driving the first portion. Loops, point-to-point, and out-
and-back rides abound, and using the Yalakom as a jump point will
undoubtedly satisfy anyone's wanderlust. The possibilities are endless.

Prospectors first ventured through this valley in the late 1800s in
search of the mother lode. Now, as we near the end of the millennium,
recreationalists are finding their way to the Yalakom. This outback pipe-
line has long served horse outfitters and hikers who have sought access
to the wilderness of the Shulaps and Camelsfoot Ranges.

Doubletrack cruising near Davey Jones Creek in the upper Yalakom

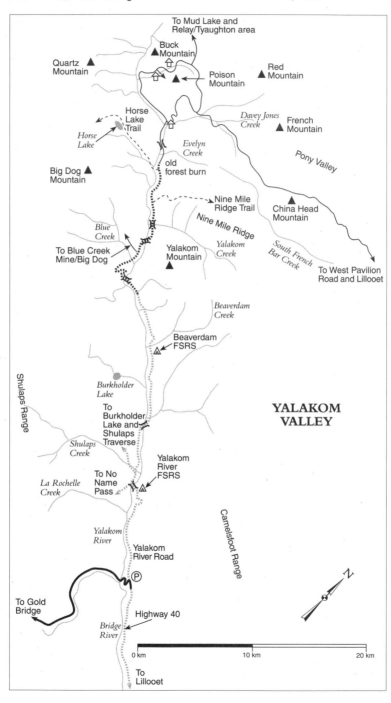

To Mud Lake and
Relay/Tyaughton area

Buck
▲Mountain

Quartz ▲
Mountain

Poison
Mountain

Red
▲ Mountain

Horse
Lake
Trail

*Davey Jones
Creek*

French
▲ Mountain

*Horse
Lake*

*Evelyn
Creek*

old
forest burn

Pony Valley

Big Dog ▲
Mountain

Nine Mile
Ridge Trail

China Head
▲ Mountain

Nine Mile Ridge

*Blue
Creek*

To Blue Creek
Mine/Big Dog

Yalakom
Mountain
▲

*Yalakom
Creek*

*South French
Bar Creek*

To West Pavilion
Road and Lillooet

*Beaverdam
Creek*

Beaverdam
△ FSRS

*Burkholder
Lake*

**YALAKOM
VALLEY**

To
Burkholder
Lake and
Shulaps
Traverse

Shulaps Range

*Shulaps
Creek*

To No
Name
Pass

Yalakom
River
FSRS
△

*La Rochelle
Creek*

*Yalakom
River*

Yalakom
River Road

Camelsfoot Range

Ⓟ

To Gold
Bridge

Highway 40

*Bridge
River*

N

0 km   10 km   20 km

To
Lillooet

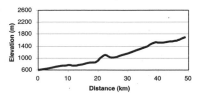

The Yalakom River Road is gravel and well maintained. The road travels north to the Poison Mountain/China Head divide that separates the southern Chilcotin from the Cariboo. Despite the inroads made by industry in recent years, the valley retains a remote atmosphere and is worth a cycling visit in itself. The loop east over China Head Mountain to the West Pavilion FSR, above the Fraser River, and back to Lillooet is highly recommended.

APPROACH

From Lillooet, head northwest on Highway 40 to Gold Bridge. At 31 kilometers (69 kilometers east of Gold Bridge if you took the Hurley Pass Road from Pemberton), turn right (north) on Yalakom River Road into the Yalakom Valley. Park here or, if on limited time, drive to any intermediate point in the valley and start there.

DISTANCE/ELEVATION LOG

0km	600m	Start of Yalakom River Road.
9.9km	730m	Yalakom River FSRS.
11.3km	740m	Option: Turn left for No Name Pass.
12.2km	750m	Stay right at Lac La Mare and head downhill for the Yalakom Valley. Option: Turn left for Burkholder Lake and Shulaps Traverse.
17.3km	850m	Stay right.
19.4km	870m	Stay right.
25.3km	1,015m	Beaverdam FSRS.
35.3km	1,340m	Option: Left turn here to Blue Creek Mine and Big Dog Mountain.
38.8km	1,520m	Cross Yalakom Creek. This is a tributary creek from Yalakom Mountain, on the east side of the valley flowing into Yalakom River.
40.8km	1,525m	Park here for Nine Mile Ridge and Horse Lake rides.
46km	1,570m	Old forest fire burn.
47km	1,630m	Yalakom River bridge.
49km	1,700m	High point of Yalakom Valley, and a junction. Option: Left will take you around the west side of Poison Mountain.

OPTION: POISON MOUNTAIN LOOP

Note: Some new logging roads in past the 49-kilometer mark toward Davey Jones Creek may have changed the access slightly.

Loop this scenic, rounded, 2,256-meter summit in about 20 kilometers. Excellent hiking potential to the summit. At 49 kilometers (1,700 meters), keep right and head uphill for an elevation gain of 300 meters over the next 3 kilometers. Drop down to Davey Jones Creek, then at the China Head junction, head left around the north side of Poison Mountain. Keep left over the pass between Poison and Buck Mountains for the loop. An optional right turn will take you west toward Mud Lake and the Relay/Tyaughton area in about 10 kilometers.

OPTION: BLUE CREEK MINE/BIG DOG MOUNTAIN

A left turn at 35.3 kilometers (1,340 meters) gives access on a steep four-by-four road (900-meter gain) to a minerally stained, unique landscape with a meadowed camping area. Hiking to the summit of Big Dog Mountain (2,900 meters) from here is rewarding. A great downhill descent.

OPTION: HORSE LAKE

At 44.5 kilometers (1,555 meters), 3.7 kilometers beyond the parking spot for Nine Mile Ridge, look for a trail to a log crossing the Yalakom River (it might be a bit tricky to find). Excellent singletrack will soon lead to Horse Lake in 2.5 kilometers. This makes for an interesting side trip.

46 NO NAME PASS

Round trip: 36km	Season: July to October
Duration: 5 hours	Terrain: DT100%
Elevation gain: 1,950m	Rating: Difficult
High point: 2,470m	Maps: 92-J/16, 92-0/1, 92-0/2

The Shulaps is the last major group of rugged mountain peaks that form the eastern boundary of the southern Chilcotin. Thanks to early mining efforts, an excellent track for mountain biking exists. No Name Pass is the first ride you will encounter as you head north up the Yalakom River valley. For those with limited time, this may be the ride to do. This out-and-back route is a classic, with excellent alpine scenery and riding that, at times, can be quite challenging. You couldn't ask for a better place to get fit. There is vehicular activity, so slow down occasionally or you could become someone's hood ornament. This somewhat strenuous cycle also provides some great hiking opportunities along the way.

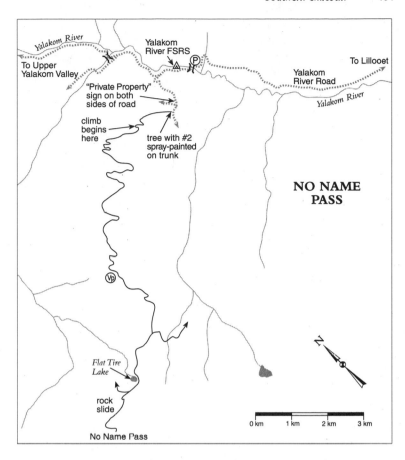

The Yalakom River FSRS is the starting point and a good place to pre-hydrate. After a 1.3-kilometer warm-up, turn left up a small side road and gently climb a short hill. The road levels through a section that can be quite muddy if it has rained recently. The mud—Chilcotin Wonder Gloop—sticks to everything, including grease and oil, so bring extra lubricant. Go right at the 3- and 3.3-kilometer marks, and left at the 4-kilometer mark, where the climb really begins. A few of the steeper pitches will have you leaning way over your handlebars. Multi-switchbacks lead to an open ridge top at 11.6 kilometers (1,890 meters), where you will want to break and drink in the views of the rounded Camelsfoot Range to the east.

Cool breezes invigorate and prompt you to continue on. A 150-meter descent leads to a saddle. Stay right and uphill and cruise the contours to Flat Tire Lake. On the map this tarn doesn't have a name,

Absorbing the scenery after fixing the puncture at Flat Tire Lake ©Tomas Vrba

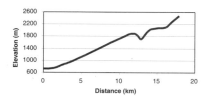

but because of the sharp rocks along the trail here and the resulting punctures, we took the liberty.

In less than a kilometer the road gets quite rough and deteriorates into a rock slide. Shoulder the bike over the worst of it; then, if you can, ride the last 300 meters of old road to the pass. Walk it if you can't; the views are worth it. The summit of No Name Pass is 2,470 meters high.

APPROACH

From Lillooet, head northwest on Highway 40 to Gold Bridge. At 31 kilometers (69 kilometers east of Gold Bridge if you took the Hurley Pass Road from Pemberton), turn right (north) on Yalakom River Road into the Yalakom Valley. Park at the Yalakom River FSRS, about 9.9 kilometers from the Highway 40 junction.

DISTANCE/ELEVATION LOG

0km	730m	At the Yalakom River FSRS, cross the river and continue up Yalakom River Road.
1.3km	740m	Turn left on a small road.
2.7km	870m	Go straight at the PRIVATE PROPERTY sign on the right.
3km	900m	Stay right and climb a short hill.
3.3km	930m	Stay right at a large tree with #2 spray-painted on its trunk.
4km	1,000m	Turn left onto a steep, narrow road. Granny-out and grind. The real climb begins here.
11.6km	1,890m	Take a break. Great views of the Shulaps Range. Prepare to descend a 200m hill, then climb back up to a junction.
14.2km	2,040m	Stay right. Follow the road through the alpine area and descend to Flat Tire Lake.
16.2km	1,950m	Pass Flat Tire Lake.
16.9km	2,070m	Turn left and climb an eroded mining road up the steep, rocky valley. Rock slide at the base of a knoll. Hike or ride the last 300m of road to the pass.
17.9km	2,470m	No Name Pass.

47 SHULAPS TRAVERSE

Point to point: 43km	Season: July to October
Duration: 6 to 8 hours	Terrain: RG45%, ST55%
Elevation gain: 1,950m	Rating: Advanced
High point: 2,250m	Maps: 92-J/16, 92-0/1, 92-0/2

Disappointment will not be in your vocabulary during this point-to-point adventure. Mountain aesthetics combined with wonderful singletrack will make you want to come back and ride this route again. Imagine cruising through kilometers of alpine on perfect, rid-able horse trail at elevations over 2,200 meters. If that doesn't satiate

The 100-kilometer Shulaps Traverse loop can take more than one day
©Tomas Vrba

your appetite, try the 1,200-meter descent down Brett Creek. This beautiful downhill singletrack will have you grinning from ear to ear by the end of the ride.

True mountain bike purists will start the traverse at the Yalakom River FSRS at the valley bottom and pedal the initial 13-kilometer, 1,000-meter elevation gain. Others may want to drive their vehicles as high as possible. Four-wheel drives should have no problem reaching the logging slash at the road's end; others may want to park when the road begins to look too rough.

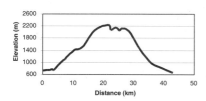

After picking up the trail in the logging slash, hike-and-bike for about an hour. At about 2,000 meters, begin a 4-kilometer jaunt through spectacular mountainscape to the high pass above Brett Creek. Prepare to become one with your bike and give yourself totally to this secret trail.

Some planning may be required if you intend to do the Shulaps Traverse as a day trip. Two vehicles are recommended; otherwise psych yourself up for a 100-kilometer loop. This is worth considering if you have never been here before. Add an extra day or so to enjoy the scenery.

APPROACH

From Lillooet, head northwest on Highway 40 to Gold Bridge. At 31 kilometers (69 kilometers east of Gold Bridge if you took the Hurley Pass Road from Pemberton), reach the Yalakom River Road

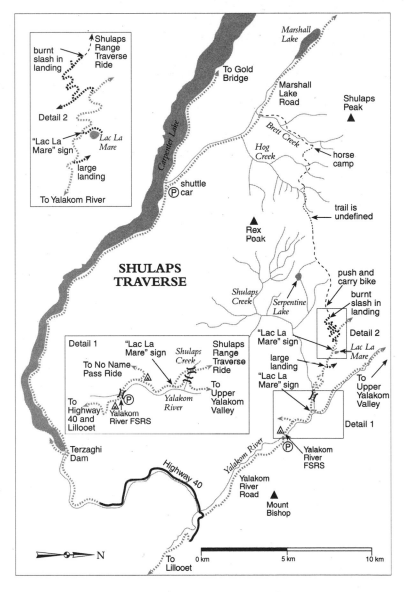

junction and turn right (north) into the Yalakom Valley. Reach the Yalakom River FSRS about 9.9 kilometers from the junction. Drive or ride the next 12 kilometers (780 vertical meters) to start the westward traverse. Park the return vehicle on Highway 40 at the Marshall Lake Road junction, 67 kilometers west of Lillooet (33 kilometers east of Gold Bridge).

DISTANCE/ELEVATION LOG

0km	730m	At the Yalakom River FSRS, cross the river and continue up Yalakom FSR.
1.3km	740m	Keep right. Option: A small road leads left to No Name Pass.
2.3km	750m	Turn left at the LAC LA MARE sign. Climb the gentle but uneven grade, enjoy a short descent to cross Shulaps Creek, and resume climbing.
6.6km	1,070m	Stay left at the large landing.
7.2km	1,110m	Stick to the main road.
7.6km	1,170m	Keep left at the LAC LA MARE sign. The road switchbacks several times.
9.9km	1,400m	Turn left at this junction and follow the branch south.
10.2km	1,410m	Turn right and climb.
13km	1,510m	The road levels and descends into the west corner of cutblock, ending at a large landing. Look for the start of the trail by the burnt slash, heading west to the treeline. Push and carry uphill for an hour. Persevere.
21.5km	2,250m	Ride over the pass. The next 7km of trail can be tricky to follow. Drop down to Hog Creek and then traverse the rolling ridge crests to Brett Creek.
28.4km	2,030m	Pass a horse camp. Trail heads left and downhill. Primo manicured singletrack.
35.1km	1,050m	Turn left on Marshall Lake Road.
43km	660m	Highway 40. Carpenter Lake. Parking for a shuttle vehicle.

48 BURKHOLDER LAKE

Round trip: 28km
Duration: 4 hours
Elevation gain: 750m
High point: 1,480m

Season: June to October
Terrain: RG55%, ST45%
Rating: Moderate
Maps: 92-J/16, 92-O/1, 92-O/2

Primo half-meter singletrack that is both interesting and scenic make this out-and-back ride a must. Expect a trail of exceptional quality with a smooth, sandy, almost manicured surface. If you were to build singletrack, the Burkholder Lake trail would certainly set the standard.

The varied scenic quality of this ride provides maximum entertainment value for your cardio output. Open ridges, spacious pine forests, and a route that wends its way along a grassy forest floor and between marshes and glades will be sure to entice. Keep a sharp eye out for moose. Huge ungulate footprints were everywhere when we rode through. Climbs are within acceptable limits; some are steep but none is technical. Views of the Shulaps and Camelsfoot Ranges are exemplary.

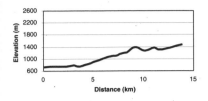

You'll reach your destination in 14 kilometers. The cool, crystal-clear waters of Burkholder Lake will beckon. Prepare to dry off in a perfect setting among the peaks and pine forest that surround the lake. If you are driven to do more, consider the ill-defined, rougher trail that heads east around the Burkholder and north to Peridotite Lake. Expect, however, a more extreme adventure, with carrying over windfalls.

The descent is swift and exciting, with the terrain melding into a blur of green and brown. Focus on the adrenaline-inducing track and think benevolently of the Lillooet mountain bikers who spent time cutting windfall to make your passage one to remember. Be aware of potential equestrian traffic and be ready to dismount. If your purist approach has wandered for the day and you simply want to cut to the chase and make room for another Chilcotin classic, use your vehicle to access.

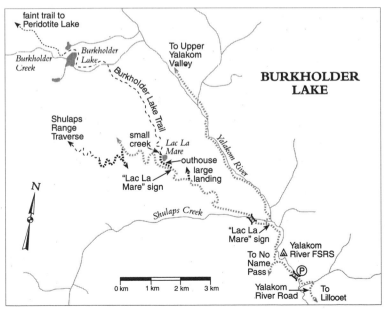

APPROACH

From Lillooet, head northwest on Highway 40 to Gold Bridge. At 31 kilometers (69 kilometers east from Gold Bridge if you took the Hurley Pass Road from Pemberton), reach the Yalakom River Road junction and turn right (north) into the Yalakom Valley. Park at the Yalakom River FSRS, about 9.9 kilometers from the junction.

DISTANCE/ELEVATION LOG

0km	730m	At the Yalakom River FSRS, cross the river and continue up Yalakom River Road.
1.3km	740m	Keep right. Option: A small road leads left to No Name Pass.
2.3km	750m	Turn left at the LAC LA MARE sign. Climb the gentle but uneven grade, enjoy a short descent to cross Shulaps Creek, and resume climbing.
6.6km	1,070m	Stay left at the large landing.
7.2km	1,110m	Stick to the main road.
7.6km	1,170m	Turn right at the LAC LA MARE sign. Follow the rough track up through the forest.
8.1km	1,200m	Lac La Mare. Pass near an outhouse and follow the road around the west side of the lake.
8.3km	1,200m	Cross a small creek and turn left onto the trail. Head through the bush and climb through mature pine forest. Super singletrack begins here.
13.9km	1,480m	Burkholder Lake. The trail is cleared for about another 2.5 kilometers.

Chain Breakage

If your chain breaks, know how to fix it. You may have to take a damaged link out or shorten the chain to make your bike into a one-speed if the derailleur breaks. When using the chain-breaking tool, do not drive the linkage pin all the way through the chain link. You'll never get the pin back in to reconnect the links. Use the chain-breaking tool to drive the pin out about 75 percent, so that about 1 mm remains on the inside of the link. This will make the reconnection easy. Flex the chain laterally after reconnection to loosen any binding that may have occurred.

Bomber singletrack riding along the shore of Burkholder Lake ©Tomas Vrba

49 NINE MILE RIDGE

Round trip:	29km	Season:	May to October
Duration:	5 hours	Terrain:	ST100%
Elevation gain:	550m	Rating:	Difficult
High point:	2,075m	Maps:	92-J/16, 92-O/1, 92-O/2

Mountain riding in a remote, high alpine environment is hard to find. One of the neatest singletrack adventures in southwest British Columbia can be experienced on Nine Mile Ridge. This sturdy horse trail traverses the Camelsfoot Range from west to east at elevations in excess of 2,000 meters. The views are expansive, covering everything in the southern Chilcotin to the Fraser Plateau.

The adventure begins in the upper Yalakom River valley at 1,525 meters and quickly ascends with some pushing into alpine regions. The travel is straightforward on rocky ground. The trail can be done as an out-and-back ride or can be made considerably longer by connecting with the China Head Mountain trail. Proficiency with a map and compass is essential, as this is outback adventure riding at its best—and most challenging. The loop can be cycled in a long day via Mosquito and South French Bar Creeks and roads that travel west toward China Head Mountain.

Wide-open, windswept singletrack riding at 2,000 meters on Nine Mile Ridge
©Tomas Vrba

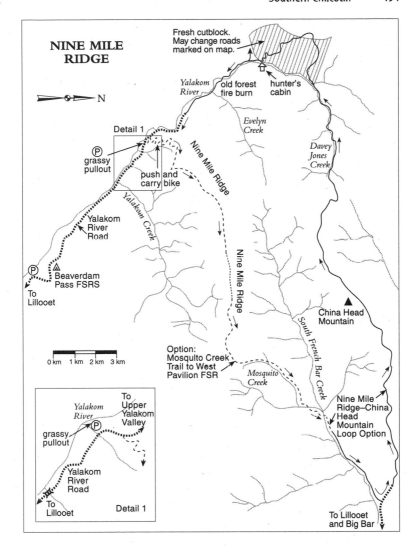

NINE MILE RIDGE

N

Fresh cutblock. May change roads marked on map.

Yalakom River / old forest fire burn   hunter's cabin

Evelyn Creek

Detail 1

(P) grassy pullout

push and carry bike

Nine Mile Ridge

Yalakom Creek

Yalakom River Road

(P) △ Beaverdam Pass FSRS

To Lillooet

Davey Jones Creek

Nine Mile Ridge

0 km 1 km 2 km 3 km

Option: Mosquito Creek Trail to West Pavilion FSR

Mosquito Creek

▲ China Head Mountain

South French Bar Creek

Nine Mile Ridge–China Head Mountain Loop Option

To Lillooet and Big Bar

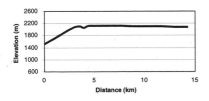

To Upper Yalakom Valley

Yalakom River

grassy pullout

(P)

Yalakom River Road

To Lillooet

Detail 1

Upon reaching the roads that connect at South French Bar Creek, you may also want to travel south to Lillooet via the West Pavilion FSR. From here it is possible to continue back to the Yalakom in an even bigger loop. You may even want to cross the Fraser at Big Bar and take the High Bar route to Lillooet. Lots of possibilities. The only constraints are time and energy.

Elevation (m)

2600
2200
1800
1400
1000
600

0   5   10   15

Distance (km)

APPROACH

From Lillooet, head northwest on Highway 40 to Gold Bridge. At 31 kilometers (69 kilometers east of Gold Bridge if you took the Hurley Pass Road from Pemberton), reach the Yalakom River Road junction and turn right (north) into the Yalakom Valley. Reach Yalakom River FSRS in 9.9 kilometers. Stay right at all junctions and pass the Beaverdam FSRS, 25.3 kilometers from the Yalakom River Road junction. At 35.3 kilometers, pass the Blue Creek Mine/Big Dog Mountain turnoff. At 38.8 kilometers, cross Yalakom Creek. Park in the grassy pullout at 40.8 kilometers from the junction for Nine Mile Ridge or Horse Lake.

DISTANCE/ELEVATION LOG

0km 1,525m From the meadow, ride 30m up the road and turn right onto a steep trail. You will have to push or carry for the next hour or so before you reach the ridge top where you can mount and ride.

3km 2,074m As you near the ridge crest, the trail will disappear. Head for the nearest clump of trees and pick up the trail again, following it east over the rolling peaks. (Make a mental note of the location of these trees for the trip down.)

14.3km 2,075m The trail drops to a narrow saddle. Option: Hike up to the peaks at the east end of the ridge, then cruise down Mosquito Creek to West Pavilion FSR.

OPTION: NINE MILE RIDGE—CHINA HEAD MOUNTAIN LOOP

Connect Nine Mile Ridge and China Head Mountain by doing a counter-clockwise loop. Follow singletrack along Mosquito Creek to a rough four-by-four road near South French Bar Creek, then join the old four-by-four track that climbs up the east side of China Head Mountain. This can be done as a light, long day. Total of 60 kilometers (about 10 hours) to return to the grassy pullout at the bottom of Nine Mile Ridge. Advanced grading.

Nuts and Bolts

Take extra nuts because they have a tendency to vibrate off. Periodically check the crank bolt in particular, because it sometimes loosens.

50 CHINA HEAD MOUNTAIN

Round trip:	80km; 49km from Nine Mile Ridge pullout	Season:	July to October
Duration:	8 hours	Terrain:	GG20%, RG20%, DT60%
Elevation gain:	1,500m	Rating:	Moderate
High point:	2,136m	Maps:	92-J/16, 92-O/1, 92-O/2

Exploration and discovery distinguish this ride. This road follows the Yalakom River deep into the dry, mineral-rich eastern ranges of the coastal mountains. It was developed as access for early miners working claims in the Poison Mountain/Blue Creek area. Today it provides a great opportunity to venture into the high alpine on primitive roads.

Past Yalakom Creek the terrain turns wild. Pass an old burn filled with contorted, bleached snags, eerie sentinels that seem to guard the way. Soon a junction is reached. Right takes you up a steep, short climb to alpine regions at 2,000 meters. Left takes you around the base of Poison Mountain. Both primitive roads meet on the east side of the

Dodging fetid, squall-like weather high on China Head Mountain

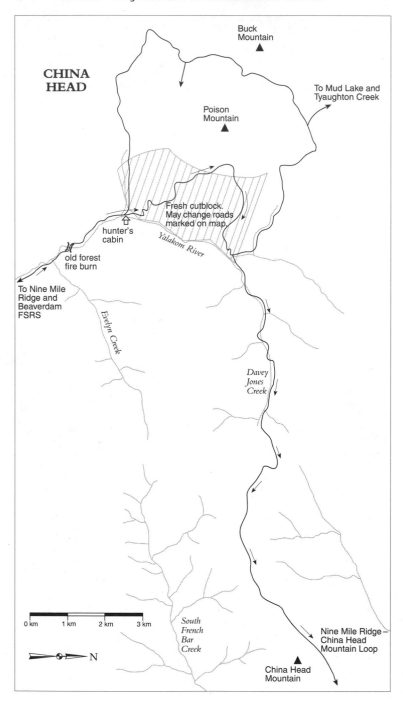

CHINA
HEAD

Buck
Mountain ▲

To Mud Lake and
Tyaughton Creek

Poison
Mountain ▲

Fresh cutblock.
May change roads
marked on map.

hunter's
cabin

Yalakom River

old forest
fire burn

To Nine Mile
Ridge and
Beaverdam
FSRS

Evelyn Creek

*Davey
Jones
Creek*

0 km   1 km   2 km   3 km

*South
French
Bar
Creek*

Nine Mile Ridge –
China Head
Mountain Loop

China Head
Mountain ▲

N

mountain and continue to the expansive, rolling ridges of China Head Mountain.

From the top of China Head Mountain (2,136 meters), the views are terrific. To the west are the mineralized peaks of the Shulaps Range; to the east, the Marble Ranges can be seen across the Fraser River. Northward, the Chilcotin stretches into the Fraser Plateau, while directly south, the Camelsfoot Range sinks into the Bridge River Valley.

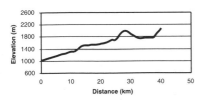

The exploration potential in this area is vast. On both the China Head ridge system and at the alpine level around Poison Mountain, hiking opportunities abound. This is also sheep range for California bighorn, so bring binoculars. Yalakom, in fact, means "ewe of the bighorn sheep."

Be careful when traveling in fragile alpine ecosystems. Do not ride off the track. The growing season is limited to a very short time because of the snowpack. This is an alpine environment and the weather can change quickly; it's a good idea to bring extra clothing.

Note: Since this area was researched, logging has pushed farther up the Yalakom Valley. Roads in the area may be slightly altered.

APPROACH

From Lillooet, head northwest on Highway 40 to Gold Bridge. At 31 kilometers (69 kilometers east of Gold Bridge if you took the Hurley Pass Road from Pemberton), reach the Yalakom River Road junction and turn right (north) into the Yalakom Valley. Reach Yalakom River FSRS in 9.9 kilometers. Stay right at all junctions and park at the Beaverdam FSRS, 25.3 kilometers from the Yalakom River Road junction. To shorten this ride, consider parking at the Nine Mile Ridge grassy pullout, 15.5 kilometers from the Beaverdam FSRS.

DISTANCE/ELEVATION LOG

0km	1,015m	Start at the Beaverdam FSRS.
10km	1,200m	Blue Creek Mine/Big Dog Mountain turnoff.
11km	1,250m	Canyon-like and bluffy.
13.5km	1,500m	Yalakom Creek bridge.
15.5km	1,525m	Start for Nine Mile Ridge to the right.
21.3km	1,570m	Old forest fire burn.
22km	1,630m	Yalakom River bridge.
23.7km	1,700m	Yalakom River Road/Poison Mountain junction. Turn right and downhill toward an old hunter's

		cabin. Option: Left will take you around the west side of Poison Mountain.
25km	1,700m	Start climbing old four-by-four road to the south flanks of Poison Mountain.
28km	2,000m	Open views, very scenic. Hiking possibility to the summit of Poison Mountain (2,256m). Descend into the Davey Jones Creek drainage.
32km	1,760m	Stay right for China Head Mountain.
37.2km	1,770m	After crossing Davey Jones Creek five times, climb toward China Head. Possible campsite.
40km	2,136m	Ride ends at a high point overlooking China Head Mountain.

OPTION: MUD LAKE AND RELAY CREEK

At the Yalakom River Road/Poison Mountain junction (23.7km/ 1,700m), turn left. After riding 11 kilometers, you will reach a rough track that leads to a crossing of Churn Creek. By continuing on this track, you can connect with the Mud Lake/Tyaughton and Relay Creek areas in about 10 additional kilometers for more riding. See the Lone Valley/Relay Creek Loop ride.

OPTION: TO LILLOOET OR BIG BAR

Continue on to Lillooet (96km) via West Pavilion FSR, or east to Big Bar (12km), crossing the Fraser River on the reaction ferry. Cycle the seldom-traveled High Bar Road (120km) along the east side of the Fraser River. Gain elevation, cross the Edge Hills to Big Bar Road, then cruise to Downing Provincial Park on Kelly Lake (camping). Continue up-hill toward Pavilion Mountain on the Pavilion/Kelly Lake Road, and then go south, back to Lillooet, on Highway 99. If you extend the ride to Lillooet, plan for a long weekend, or add an extra day to continue the ride on the Big Bar/Kelly Lake segment.

Appendices

USEFUL TECHNIQUES FOR TECHNICAL TERRAIN

Anticipation

You will benefit greatly if you learn to anticipate. Familiarity with the event field and its terrain will give you an advantage in preparing for the moves ahead. This will ultimately make the difference between scooting through in one fluid move and hesitating in an off-balanced quandary. Start by riding with a few obstacles in your path, then, as your comfort level increases, add more obstacles to quicken your reaction time. Anticipation is key and will help you surmount any obstacle. This is the first step in becoming one with your steel steed.

Bunny Hop

This fun move will help you bike over low obstacles with ease. It is performed, while moving, by focusing all energy in the arms and legs downward, then evenly and dynamically pulling up with both arms and legs. The idea is to use some of the bounce in the tires to help the bike lift off the ground. At speed, this technique is especially useful in avoiding potholes, small rocks, and fallen branches.

Front-wheel Hop

The front-wheel hop is one of the easiest mountain biking moves to learn. It is used for jumping small obstacles like curbs or small logs. Focus your energy on the front of the bike, then lift the bars with your arms to dynamically pop the front wheel over the obstacle.

Rear-wheel Hop

The rear-wheel hop is more technically advanced and takes practice to master. Stop the bike with the front brakes, then use the power in your legs to lift and swivel the back tire around an obstacle. Sound easy? On steep terrain this technique can be a real asset. It is especially useful on sharp-cornered switchbacks. This stylish move may make the difference between cleaning the trail and not.

Log-hopping Crampon Technique

The bigger a log is, the harder it is to navigate. On some logs, a basic front-wheel hop won't be sufficient for clearance, although the technique will be needed as a prerequisite. For the log-hopping crampon technique, more energy is required to lift the front tire higher, to high-center the bike on the log. The chain ring will embed itself in the log. Here lies the skill. You must then use a power-stroke with the forward inertia of the moving bike to pop over the log. It's tricky. You have to use some upper body strength in combination with the downward pedal stroke. The key is to keep the bike moving and not to stop. Try to keep in balance and don't buck yourself off the bike in the process.

Canting

This advanced balance technique is useful in navigating terrain littered with multiple obstacles. It combines body and bike movement, where the body is "canted" off the bike by as much as 45 degrees. To do this, you are always off the seat and standing on your pedals, moving your bike and body, finding the center of gravity to keep in balance. This movement helps bend your bike around rough terrain. It is a particularly good technique when moving through trees or around large rocks.

Ratcheting

This is another advanced technique for multiple-obstacle terrain that might otherwise interfere with a full pedal stroke. Standing on your pedals, pedal downward in continuous quick, short strokes. Try to keep your balance. When the terrain is full of clutter this may be the only reasonable way to progress.

Crashing

An art unto itself, learning how to crash can be an asset. The primary rule is to leave the bike. The bike is strong and will withstand major impact. If you stay with the bike, it will likely cause a big hurt when on impact you find yourself pinned between the obstacle and the bike. Learn to fall on your shoulders and roll. This will safely disperse the energy of the fall. If you try to stop your fall using your arms or hands, you will likely break them. If your need for speed is important, learn to fall safely.

METERS TO FEET EQUIVALENTS

100 meters	357 feet
200 meters	714 feet
300 meters	1,071 feet
400 meters	1,428 feet
500 meters	1,785 feet
600 meters	2,142 feet
700 meters	2,499 feet
800 meters	2,856 feet
900 meters	3,213 feet
1000 meters	3,570 feet
2000 meters	7,140 feet
3000 meters	10,710 feet
1 mile	1.61 kilometers
1 kilometer	0.6211 mile
1 kilometer	1,000 meters

Resting on the "smooooth" Relay Creek Valley mining/logging road

RIDES BY DIFFICULTY

RIDE	EASY	MODERATE	DIFFICULT	ADVANCED
SQUAMISH				
1. Marion and Phyllis Lakes	●			
Furry Creek		●		
2. Squamish to Indian Arm		●		
3. Ring Creek Rip		●		
Powerhouse Plunge			●	
4. Powersmart			●	
5. Elfin Lakes	●			
6. Alice Lake Provincial Park	●			
7. Brohm Ridge			●	
8. Cheakamus Canyon		●		
9. Squamish and Elaho River Valleys	●			
WHISTLER/PEMBERTON				
10. Chance Creek to Function Junction	●			
11. Cheakamus Lake	●			
12. Black Tusk			●	
13. Green Lake Loop		●		
Thrill Me Kill Me			●	
14. Cougar Mountain/Ancient Cedar Grove	●			
15. Lillooet River Loop		●		
Overnight Sensation			●	
16. Birkenhead Lake	●			
17. Old Douglas Trail		●		
18. Blowdown Pass		●		
FRASER VALLEY				
19. Golden Ears Canyon	●			
20. Upper Pitt River	●			
21. Blue Mountain Ridge		●		
22. Wahleach Lake	●			
23. Harrison Lake East	●			
24. Clear Creek Hot Springs			●	
25. Chehalis River–Harrison Lake Loop		●		

RIDE	EASY	MODERATE	DIFFICULT	ADVANCED
CHILLIWACK RIVER VALLEY				
26. Mount Thurston/Mount Mercer Loop		●		
27. Chilliwack Lake Eastside Road	●			
28. Centre Creek Valley	●			
29. Nesakwatch Creek Valley	●			
30. Vedder Mountain Loop	●			
Vedder Mountain Singletrack		●		
SIMILKAMEEN				
31. Trapper Lake			●	
32. Placer Mountain		●		
33. Placer Lake		●		
34. Lodestone Mountain/Badger Creek Loop			●	
35. Windy Joe		●		
36. Monument 83		●		
LILLOOET				
37. Lytton to Lillooet		●		
38. Molybdenite Lake			●	
39. Botanie Mountain			●	
40. Watson Bar Creek Loop		●		
SOUTHERN CHILCOTIN				
41. Gold Bridge/Bralorne Loop	●			
42. Gun Creek to Spruce Lake		●		
43. Taylor Pass		●		
44. Lone Valley–Relay Creek Loop			●	
45. Yalakom Valley		●		
46. No Name Pass			●	
47. Shulaps Traverse				●
48. Burkholder Lake		●		
49. Nine Mile Ridge			●	
50. China Head Mountain		●		

Glossary

Bivy Camping without a tent
Bomber Excellent, solid, the best
Bonk General collapse; horking possible
Buff Super-good trail with few obstacles
Bunny hop While riding a bike, hopping it over an obstacle such as a rock, log, or pothole
Chunky Fist-size boulders on the road
Cirque Steep mountain wall that experiences constant erosion by snow and ice
Clean To ride a trail without dismounting; considered good style
Cutblock Small section of cut forest; not a clearcut
Doubletrack Old road, usually four-by-four, sometimes driveable
Doughnut Cowpie
Fetid Conditions that are inclement or slimy, from weather to rotten food
Ford Creek crossing, usually carrying the bike
FSR Forest Service Road
FSRS Forest Service Recreation Site
Glacial flour Glacially ground powdered rock, often suspended in water
Gonzo A "Go for it" attitude
Granny Lowest gear
Grind Uphill pedal with some sweat
Gut-wrench Struggling for air; expect dehydration, malaise
Hike-and-bike Pushing or carrying the bike over unpedalable ground
Honed Being at one with or on top of your sport
Hoodoo Pillars of old river and glacial deposition, composed of sand, gravel, and mud
Hork Basic upchuck
Miscreant General deviant who preys upon unguarded or unlocked possessions
Non-nuclear riding Easy riding or hike-and-biking
Pigging out Eating copious amounts of food for energy
Singletrack Narrow trail
Superman Being launched over the handlebars
Talus Scree slope caused by erosion
Test piece A ride that is at or just beyond your technical limit
Waterbars Open drainage ditches that cross logging roads to prevent erosion

Bibliography

A Guide to Climbing and Hiking in Southwestern British Columbia, Bruce Fairley. Vancouver, Soules Publishing: 1987.

Mountaineering: The Freedom of the Hills, 6th Edition. Seattle, The Mountaineers: 1997.

Introduction to Physical Geography, Arthur Strahler. New York, Wiley Press: 1995.

Lower Mainland Backroads, Richard Wright. Sydney, B.C., Saltaire Publishing/BC Outdoors: 1977.

Medicine for Mountaineering, James A. Wilkerson. Seattle, The Mountaineers: 1992.

Mountain Bike, W. Nealy. San Francisco, Velo Press: 1996.

Plants and Animals of the Pacific Northwest, 7th Edition, Eugene Kozloff. Vancouver, Greystone Press: 1995.

Zinn and the Art of Mountain Bike Maintenance, 2nd Edition, Lennard Zinn. San Francisco, Velo Press: 1996.

The Complete Book of Mountain Biking, Richards and Worland. New York, HarperCollins: 1997.

Index

About the Author

Greg Maurer is a professional writer/photographer specializing in adventurous outdoor recreation (hiking, climbing, kayaking, skiing, rafting, trail running). He has been widely published in numerous Canadian magazines, including *Equinox, Beautiful BC, Powder, Bike, Coast, Canadian Airlines, Vancouver Sun,* and *BC Outdoors.* He's also contributed photographs for a number of coffee table publications.

In addition to researching this guide, Greg has used the mountain bike to tour extensively in the mountainous regions of western Canada. His cycling destinations have included the Canadian Rockies, B.C.'s Coast Mountains, the Yukon, the Northwest Territories, and Washington State.

Greg Maurer ©Kerry Dawson

THE MOUNTAINEERS, founded in 1906, is a nonprofit outdoor activity and conservation club, whose mission is "to explore, study, preserve, and enjoy the natural beauty of the outdoors. . . . " Based in Seattle, Washington, the club is now the third-largest such organization in the United States, with 15,000 members and five branches throughout Washington State.

The Mountaineers sponsors both classes and year-round outdoor activities in the Pacific Northwest, which include hiking, mountain climbing, ski-touring, snowshoeing, bicycling, camping, kayaking and canoeing, nature study, sailing, and adventure travel. The club's conservation division supports environmental causes through educational activities, sponsoring legislation, and presenting informational programs. All club activities are led by skilled, experienced volunteers, who are dedicated to promoting safe and responsible enjoyment and preservation of the outdoors.

If you would like to participate in these organized outdoor activities or the club's programs, consider a membership in The Mountaineers. For information and an application, write or call The Mountaineers, Club Headquarters, 300 Third Avenue West, Seattle, Washington 98119; (206) 284-6310.

The Mountaineers Books, an active, nonprofit publishing program of the club, produces guidebooks, instructional texts, historical works, natural history guides, and works on environmental conservation. All books produced by The Mountaineers are aimed at fulfilling the club's mission.

Send or call for our catalog of more than 300 outdoor titles:

 The Mountaineers Books
1001 SW Klickitat Way, Suite 201
Seattle, WA 98134
1-800-553-4453
e-mail: mbooks@mountaineers.org
website: www.mountaineersbooks.org

Other titles you may enjoy from The Mountaineers:

CONDITIONING FOR OUTDOOR FITNESS:
A Comprehensive Training Guide, *David Musnick, M.D. & Sandy Elliot, P.T. with Mark Pierce, A.T.C.*
The most comprehensive guide to conditioning, fitness, and training for *all* outdoor activities, featuring a "whole body" approach by experts in the field. Includes training programs for hiking, biking, skiing, climbing, paddling, and more.

BICYCLING WITH CHILDREN: A Complete How-To Guide,
Trudy E. Bell with Roxana K. Bell
Everything a parent needs to know about bikes and kids, from toddlers to teens: good features for a parent's bicycle; teaching kids to ride; teaching traffic safety; buying and caring for children's bikes; cycling for children with special challenges; and much more.

MOUNTAIN BIKE ADVENTURES IN™ Series
Complete guides to off-road cycling in the Four Corners region, the Northern Rockies, and Washington's North and South Cascades—five titles in all.

103 HIKES IN SOUTHWESTERN BRITISH COLUMBIA,
Fourth Edition, *David & Mary Macaree*
An updated and revised guide covering Lytton in the north, and from Vancouver Island east to Manning Park.

THE WEST COAST TRAIL AND OTHER GREAT HIKES,
Eighth Edition, *Tim Leadem*
Detailed, thoroughly updated guide to Vancouver Island's increasingly popular West Coast Trail, from Bamfield to Port Renfrew.

BICYCLING THE PACIFIC COAST: A Complete Route Guide,
Canada to Mexico, *Tom Kirkendall & Vicky Spring*
A complete road guide for trip planning and touring along the entire Pacific Coast.

BIKING THE GREAT NORTHWEST: 20 Tours in Washington,
Oregon, Idaho, and Montana, *Jean Henderson*
Multi-day tours, many of them loops, for great Northwest cycling vacations.